# THE WILDEST COUNTRY
## EXPLORING THOREAU'S MAINE

J. Parker Huber

Photographs by Bridget Besaw

APPALACHIAN MOUNTAIN CLUB BOOKS
BOSTON, MASSACHUSETTS

The AMC is a nonprofit organization and sales of AMC books fund our mission of protecting the Northeast outdoors. If you appreciate our efforts and would like make a donation to AMC Books, contact us at Appalachian Mountain Club Books, 5 Joy Street, Boston, MA 02108.

http://www.outdoors.org/publications/books/

Cover design by Eric Edstam
Interior design by Jennie Sparrow
Front cover photograph and chapter-opener photographs © Bridget Besaw
Back cover photograph courtesy of the Thoreau Institute at Walden Woods

Distributed by The Globe Pequot Press, Guilford, Connecticut.

Huber, J. Parker.
  The wildest country : exploring Thoreau's Maine / J. Parker Huber. —2nd ed.
     p. cm.
  Includes bibliographical references and index.
  ISBN 978-1-934028-09-4 (alk. paper)
  1. Thoreau, Henry David, 1817–1862—Homes and haunts—Maine. 2. Literary landmarks—Maine. 3. Maine—Description and travel. I. Title.
  PS3053.H79 2008
  818'.303—dc22
  [B]
                              2008003936

The paper used in this publication meets the minimum requirements of the American National Standard for Information Sciences—Permanence of Paper for Printed Library Materials, ANSI Z39.48-1984. ∞

Due to changes in conditions, use of the information in this book is at the sole risk of the user.

Printed in Canada.

Printed on 10% post-consumer recycled fiber.

9 8 7 6 5 4 3 2 1          08 09 10 11 12 13 14 15 16

## An Invitation

This book is an invitation. It invites you to gain an appreciation of yourself, Maine, and Thoreau. It invites you to follow Thoreau's travels on foot and by canoe. It invites you to see the North Woods through the eyes of Thoreau, who, in my opinion, is still that region's interpreter extraordinary, and it asks you to compare and contrast his perceptions with yours. It invites your additions and criticisms. It invites itself to be part of your journey, to be read as you go along. It invites you to be stimulated by this world. Lastly, it invites you to conserve and cherish the land and wildlife. Though the country has changed since the mid-nineteenth century, its character remains the same for you as it did for Thoreau. It is still a frontier for the mind, heart, and spirit.

J. Parker Huber

In loving memory of
**William Ceylon Crewson**
(1896–1967)


*Forever when I think of the north woods,*
*Bill will be paddling across Otter Lake—*
*Faded blue shirt, red hair, burly chest—*
*Its surface reflecting moments we shared:*
*Canoe-tripping summers, wood-splitting falls,*
*Ice-cutting winters, bean-planting springs.*

*How gently he showed me,*
*How quietly he inspired me,*
*How deeply he touched me.*

*The north woods preserves his spirit and his love.*
*That is why I shall always return.*

# Contents

## FOREWORD

What a gift to have a new edition of J. Parker Huber's *The Wildest Country*, and so be able to continue the intellectual lineage that stretches back to Henry Thoreau (and Joe Polis). For more than a century and a half, Americans have been learning deep lessons from these woods and mountains and lakes, filtered through extraordinary minds and hearts. And now we need those lessons more than ever.

In an age of utter environmental chaos, with ice caps suddenly disappearing before our eyes and our oceans starting an ominous rise, there's something incredibly calming about being able still to follow Thoreau's journey—to be able to follow it literally, along the new Thoreau-Wabanaki canoe trail, through the cool shade of the pines hugging the shorelines. And to be able to follow it spiritually, through the lens of his remarkable mind.

As always, Thoreau was far ahead of his time. (It's no wonder that nobody read him in his day—it's hard to imagine how they could have made much sense of what he had to say.) He was writing for a people as sapped of meaning as ourselves, people so disconnected from place and nature that abstractions like Google have come to seem like homes. Thoreau wanted reality—he wanted bedrock, to wiggle his toes down through the muck until he touched bottom. "*Contact!*" as he all but screamed in his accounts.

It's that contact we require, too—a grounding in reality that wakes us up from the seductive consumer enchantment we've slumbered through these last decades. Sometimes that reality is harsh: *everything frozen is melting.* Sometimes it's sweet: the sun drying the water off your back after a mid-summer dip in a bracing cold lake. But always it's ennobling. We were meant to deal with reality—that's why we have the big brain and the big heart.

This is a guidebook into that reality. It will tell you how to get there—which fork to take, where to pitch the tent. And it will tell you, at least a little, how to take it in. You could ask for no better guides than Huber and Thoreau. If you get lost, it will be the good kind of lost.

Bill McKibben

## INTRODUCTION

*"I need to go to Moosehead every afternoon, & camp out every night."*
—Henry D. Thoreau, Letter, August 25, 1859

*"Katahdin is the best mountain in the wildest wild to be had on this side of the continent."*
—*Theodore Winthrop,* Life in the Open Air

It is a pleasure to welcome readers to this new edition of *The Wildest Country: Exploring Thoreau's Maine,* twenty-seven years after it was first published.

The Maine woods have inspired many—tourists, pilgrims, loggers, hunters, and anglers. They have excited a sense of adventure and well-being. They have stirred the creative imagination. It is possible that no one was more stirred than Thoreau. And the power of his prose continues to enrich the experience of this landscape.

"Think of our life in nature—daily to be shown matter, to come in contact with it—rocks, trees, wind on our cheeks! the *solid* earth! the *actual* world! the *common sense! Contact! Contact!"* Henry David Thoreau exclaimed upon Katahdin, in September 1846. His exhilaration served as a call to others to come and see what meaning their connection with this "wildest country" held for them.

This book had its origin in Maine. Six of us, following Benedict Arnold's trail to Quebec by canoe, were camped along the Kennebec River. As we talked by the fire, one of the group, Frank Couvares, mentioned Thoreau and asked if he had been here. I did not know. After arriving home, I studied Thoreau's *The Maine Woods* and mapped out where he went. His travels immediately appealed to me, as both a wilderness and a learning experience. The next summer, 1974, James H. Fox and I offered a seminar on Thoreau in which we retraced 330 miles of his journeys in Maine.

The need for a guidebook to the area was apparent from the start. In 1975, I submitted a draft to the Appalachian Mountain Club, which was not then able to act. Three years elapsed. Then, out of the blue the encouraging voice of the Club's new Director of Publications, Arlyn S. Powell, Jr., greeted me over the phone with the proposal to publish. Discussions ensued in which a new format for the book emerged. I began to work on it on September 1, 1979. The first edition was published two years later.

Will you be next to come into the Maine woods? If so, you will encounter changes from what the first edition of *The Wildest Country* described. Throughout this new edition, I have provided updates on some of the people and places I discussed then. Where necessary, trail and river descriptions have also been updated to reflect changes in land ownership and use.

Our consciousness has also changed. Now we come into the Maine woods with a fresh awareness, mindful that our interaction with our environment matters greatly. How we move from one place to another makes a significant difference. Consider how you travel and how that affects nature. Most will come to Maine by car. However, you can take public transportation for part of the journey. Since December 15, 2001, passenger train service has been restored. Amtrak's Downeaster smoothly transports you from Boston to Portland in two-and-a-half hours. Moreover, each year many arrive in the heart of the wildest country on foot via the Appalachian Trail. Others now are paddling through the region on the Northern Forest Canoe Trail, which officially opened in June 2006, and duplicates Thoreau's passage from Moosehead to Eagle lakes.

Since my journey in the Maine woods, awareness of the historical and environmental significance of this region has increased. To help preserve this area and honor Thoreau's travels, an organization called Maine Woods Forever established the Thoreau-Wabanaki Trail. It traces Thoreau's route—the one you will read about in these pages. It officially opened in July 2007; you can learn more by visiting www.thoreauwabanakitrail.org.

Some may decide not to explore the Maine woods. In the mid-1990s I felt called to let go of the Maine woods, to let them renew and replenish. A spiritual realization came to me intuitively—that this was the time for my Maine wilderness travels to stop. It came during my three-year period of car consciousness, wherein I drove my car only once a week if necessary. In 1996, I sold my car and have been carless ever since. So I have not been back since July 1995. Like Thoreau, I still dwell there spiritually: paddling Moosehead Lake, climbing Kineo and Katahdin, watching moose, listening to loons.

Whether we choose to be in the Maine woods or not, we are still asked to be stewards of this treasured landscape. Our task, as Thoreau wished, is to preserve life, not destroy it. Maine is, as Ian Marshall wrote of Katahdin, "the gift of the world."

J. Parker Huber
P.O. Box 360
Brattleboro, VT 05302
August 1, 2007

## ACKNOWLEDGMENTS

Over the years many people have helped with this endeavor. I thank you all, even though it is impossible to recognize each one of you individually. Be assured, however, that any mistakes that remain herein are mine, not yours.

I am indebted to Arlyn S. Powell, the Director of Publications of the Appalachian Mountain Club when *The Wildest Country* was first published, for his nourishment of the project. I am also grateful to Charles R. Webb, the former President of Eastern Connecticut State College, for his continued encouragement of my work, and to the Board of Trustees of the Connecticut State Colleges for providing a leave of absence during which I completed the text.

This book would not have been possible without the aid of the following librarians who worked at the corresponding libraries during my work on the first edition: Joan Lucia and Jody Newmyer, Eastern Connecticut State College Library; Kay Littlefield and Sue Wright, Bangor Public Library; Cynthia Murphy and Esta J. Astor, Maine Historical Society; Maggie Holtzberg, Olin Library, Wesleyan University; Linda E. McLean, Olana State Historic Site; Sheila L. Alexander, Portland Public Library; Shirley Thayer, Maine State Library, Yale University; Eric S. Flower, Fogler Library, University of Maine at Orono; Douglas W. Marshall, William L. Clements Library, University of Michigan; Mary Jo Pugh, Bentley Historical Library, University of Michigan; Linda Hubbard, Shaw Public Library, Greenville, Maine; Constance Holling, Brewer Public Library; and Joyce T. Woodman and Marcia Moss, Concord Free Public Library.

This guide has benefited immeasurably from a distinguished group of naturalists who have identified species, answered questions, and reviewed sections (they worked at the following institutions when the first edition was published): Arthur J. Boucot, Professor of Geology, Oregon State University; Helen Cruickshank; Francis D. Dunn, Maine Department of Inland Fisheries and Wildlife; Phillip F. Elliott, Assistant Professor of Biology, Eastern Connecticut State College; Craig W. Greene, Faculty Member in Botany, College of the Atlantic; Fay Hyland, Professor Emeritus of Botany, University of Maine at Orono; Amr A. Ismail, Associate Professor and Blueberry Specialist, University of Maine at Orono; Glenn C. Prescott Jr., Supervisory Hydrologist, United Sates Geological Survey, Augusta, Maine; Robert Prescott, Education Director, Cape Cod Museum of Natural History; Randolph L. Peterson, Curator-in-Charge, Mammalogy, Royal Ontario Museum; and Scott A. Sutcliffe, Director, Loon Preservation Committee, Audubon Society of New Hampshire.

A celebrated coterie of Thoreau scholars has been helpful to me as it has to so many others: Walter Harding, Anne R. McGrath, Thomas Blanding, and Leonard N. Neufeldt.

Robert N. Haskell deserves special recognition for an understanding of the Maine woods that he carefully imparted to me.

Other authorities on Maine also contributed: Judith Sanders Sanborn of Greenville; Mrs. Joseph Sewall of Orono; David T. Sewall and Glenn Starbird Jr. of Old Town; James B. Vickery of Brewer; Deborah Thompson and Anita Kurth of Bangor; Richard F. Dole of South Portland; Charles G. Bolté of Dresden; Dorothy B. Laverty; Marion Whitney Smith; Paul K. McCann, Manager of Public Affairs, Great Northern Paper Company; Irvin C. Caverly Jr., Supervisor, Baxter State Park, Millinocket; and Richard S. Sprague, Professor of English, University of Maine at Orono.

I also appreciate the assistance of Richard E. Slavin III of the New York State Historical Association for information on Frederic Edwin Church, and of Elizabeth Maxfield Miller of Concord for her knowledge of Edward S. Hoar.

For this second edition, research to uncover the historical photos was provided by Becky Fullerton. David Cooper and Mike Hermann served as cartographers. Arlyn Powell edited the manuscript for the first edition, and Dan Eisner, the Appalachian Mountain Club's current Books Editor, helped update it. Bryan Davidson oversaw production.

I owe a great deal to those who have participated in my "Thoreau's Maine Woods" summer seminars, many of whom still keep in touch. Their memories still light the trail.

It was a very wonderful person who labored physically, mentally, and emotionally to prepare me for the first of these adventures. Although she and I are no longer together, Jan's enrichment of this program will never be forgotten.

I am also grateful for the Quimby Family Foundation's support in making this new edition possible. Maine Woods Forever graciously provided their map of the Thoreau-Wabanaki Trail. For help with some of the new information, I am indebted to Dean Bennett of Mount Vernon, Maine; Martina Dancing of Brattleboro, Vermont; Candy Canders Russell, Director of the Moosehead Historical Society in Greenville, Maine; Richard E. Winslow III of Rye, New Hampshire; and all the authors whose writings informed this text. It was a great gift to have Sarah J. Rabkin of Soquel, California, and Susan Pollack of Gloucester, Massachusetts edit this manuscript. As always I welcome your comments.

## A NOTE ON REFERENCES

This book relies on previous scholars for whom I am most grateful. All authorities are acknowledged. To limit repetitions, shortcuts are taken. Usually, when clear, sources for subjects discussed in the text are given in the Further Reading section at the end of the book. When the reference is not obvious, a footnote is included. The excellent edition of *The Maine Woods* edited by Joseph J. Moldenhauer and published by Princeton University Press in 1972 is drawn on most frequently. References to it are identified by page number, which appear at the end of the quotation in parentheses. Alas, the edition of Thoreau's *Journal* published by Princeton University Press was not available before I finished; hence the 1906 edition of his *Journal* edited by Bradford Torrey and Francis H. Allen and republished by Dover Publications in 1962 has been used; quotations from it are identified by date.

A few common abbreviations were necessary. They are DAB for *Dictionary of American Biography*, MFS for Maine Forest Service, USGS for United States Geological Survey, and ANB for American National Biography.

*You must love the crust of the earth on which you dwell*
*more than the sweet crust of any bread or cake.*
*You must be able to extract nutriment out of a sandheap.*
*You must have so good an appetite as this,*
*else you will live in vain.*
    —*Henry David Thoreau, January 25, 1858*

*The country is an archipelago of lakes,—the lake-country of New England. (36)*

## CHAPTER 1
# Thoreau and Maine

## Itinerary for Inquiry

Thoreau's association with Maine spanned two decades. He spent over nine weeks there at different times in the mid-nineteenth century. He came first in May 1838 looking for a teaching position, but he found instead a lifelong fascination with Maine's interior. This he returned to explore with rivermen in a bateau and Penobscot Indians in birchbark canoes. Bangor was his point of departure. From there in 1846, he traveled to Katahdin and back via the Penobscot River and its West Branch. His next excursion came in 1853, when he went from Bangor to Greenville, across Moosehead Lake, and down the West Branch to Chesuncook Lake before returning to his starting point. His last and longest voyage, occurring four years later, took him again to Chesuncook and from there by the Allagash Lakes, East Branch, and Penobscot back to Bangor.[1]

The impression of these experiences was indelible. Thoreau talked about them for the rest of his life; reputedly, his final words were "moose" and "Indians."[2] He delivered lectures and wrote essays about each trip.[3] "Ktaadn" was published by the *Union Magazine of Literature and Art* in 1848, and ten years later *Atlantic Monthly* featured "Chesuncook." The third essay, "The Allegash and East Branch," did not appear in print until after Thoreau's death. Combined with the two earlier pieces, it formed a trilogy called *The Maine Woods,* the first edition of which was published in 1864.[4]

*The Maine Woods* is the primary source for establishing Thoreau's course of travel. Because he tells us exactly where he went, we are able to follow along. His three sojourns are considered here as one circuit from Moosehead Lake to Katahdin, adding the Penobscot River as the final leg. The overland segment between Bangor and Greenville is omitted. (Thoreau saw little of this country because rain fell every time he made the trip.) As you will see, Thoreau's travels blend beautifully into one grand tour of some of Maine's most impressive scenery; it can be enjoyed for a day, a week, or a lifetime.

This guide divides his route into geographical regions which can be explored separately or with as many others as you wish. To help with your trip, a comprehensive map and summaries of Thoreau's

*. . . not only for strength, but for beauty, the poet must, from time to time, travel the logger's path and the Indian's trail, to drink at some new and more bracing fountain of the Muses, far in the recesses of the wilderness. (156)*

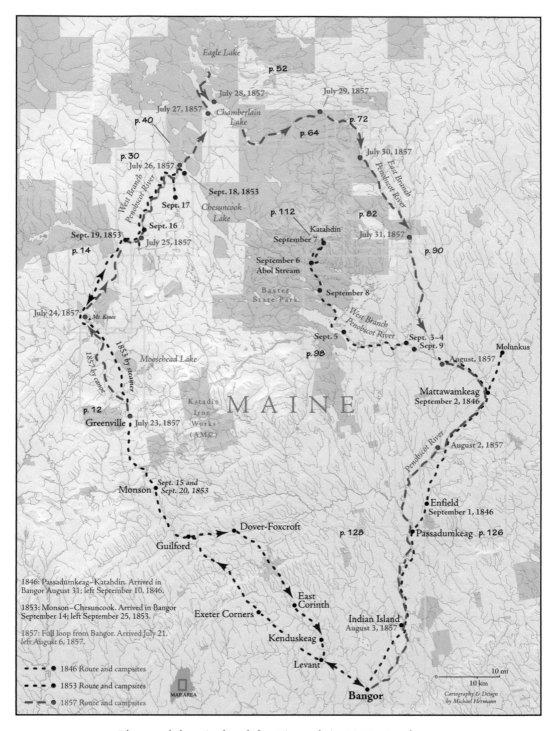

*Eagle Lake*

p. 52

July 28, 1857

July 27, 1857

July 29, 1857

p. 40

*Chamberlain Lake*

p. 72

p. 64

July 30, 1857

p. 30

July 26, 1857

*East Branch Penobscot River*

Sept. 18, 1853

*West Branch Penobscot River*

Sept. 17

p. 112

p. 82

Sept. 16

*Chesuncook Lake*

Katahdin

July 31, 1857

Sept. 19, 1853

September 7

July 25, 1857

September 6
Abol Stream

p. 90

p. 14

September 8

*Baxter State Park*

July 24, 1857   • *Mt. Kineo*

*West Branch Penobscot River*

September 8

Sept. 5

Sept. 3–4
Sept. 9

Molunkus

*1853 by steamer*

*Moosehead Lake*

p. 98

August, 1857

*1857 by canoe*

*Katadin Iron Works (AMC)*

M A I N E

Mattawamkeag
September 2, 1846

p. 12

Greenville   July 23, 1857

*Penobscot River*

August 2, 1857

Monson   Sept. 15 and
Sept. 20, 1853

Enfield
September 1, 1846

Dover-Foxcroft

p. 128

Passadumkeag   p. 126

Guilford

East
Corinth

1846: Passadumkeag–Katahdin. Arrived in
Bangor August 31; left September 10, 1846.

Exeter Corners

Indian Island
August 3, 1857

1853: Monson–Chesuncook. Arrived in Bangor
September 14; left September 25, 1853.

Kenduskeag

1857: Full loop from Bangor. Arrived July 21,
left August 6, 1857.

Levant

- - - •   1846 Route and campsites

- - - •   1853 Route and campsites

─ ─ •   1857 Route and campsites

MAP AREA

Bangor

0          10 mi
0    10 km

*Cartography & Design
by Michael Hermann*

*Thoreau took three trips through the Maine woods: in 1846, 1853, and 1857.
See the corresponding pages for detailed maps.*

*View of the city of Bangor, circa 1870*

itineraries are provided on the following pages. Each chapter following then discusses a segment of his route, including, where pertinent, the past and present landscape and social and natural history. Related readings, places of interest, and regional maps are also included.

## Down East Traveler

### WHY DID THOREAU GO TO MAINE?

He went in part because at the core of his being he was a traveler.[5] As he wrote in *Walden,* "I have traveled a good deal in Concord,"—and he might have added "in New England," for he had toured its fields, swamps, mountains, and coast. He was not a typical tourist, who stays at modern motels and stops briefly along the road to look at what is marked as "scenic views," then drives on more enamored of mileage than beauty. No, Thoreau was quite different.

His travels had a distinctive style. He moved at his own pace, usually on foot or by boat. He loved to walk. He preferred to be alone, though in Maine he welcomed company. He traveled light. He inspected whatever caught his fancy, taking notes which he expanded upon returning home.

Thoreau also roamed vicariously and imaginatively. To "live at home like a traveler" was his creed; travel literature, his passion.[6] He relished the discoveries of others as much as his own. He accompanied Charles Darwin in the South Pacific, Mungo Park in Africa, and Elisha Kane in the Arctic. No continent was too remote, no trek too arduous for his intellect. With feet fixed, his mind migrated across America with Lewis and Clark.

His greatest pleasure was to join physical and mental travels. His ramblings stimulated his research and vice versa. *The Maine Woods,* thus, is embellished with observations of others who had been there before him: England's John Montresor, engineer, and John Josselyn, naturalist; French botanist F. André Michaux; various Jesuits; Maine lumberman John S. Springer; geologist Charles T. Jackson; and other Yankees.

## BIOLOGICAL JOURNEY

> *. . . I wished to see a moose near at hand. . . . (99)*

Thoreau also went because he was intensely curious about his surroundings. He wanted to know the natural history of Maine. *The Maine Woods* faithfully records the animals, birds, and plants that he saw. Many were familiar; a few, new—jack pines, swamp birch, and a species of goldenrod.

**Thoreau's Katahdin Trip, 1846, with George A. Thatcher, Thomas Fowler Jr., and Others**

| Date | From | Via | To |
|---|---|---|---|
| August 31, Monday | Concord, Mass. <br> Boston | train <br> steamer | Boston <br> Bangor, Maine |
| September 1 | Bangor <br> Old Town <br> Milford | horse & buggy <br> bateau <br> horse & buggy | Old Town <br> Milford <br> Enfield |
| September 2 | Enfield <br> Mattawamkeag <br> Molunkus | horse & buggy <br> horse & buggy <br> horse & buggy | Mattawamkeag <br> Molunkus <br> Mattawamkeag |
| September 3 | Mattawamkeag | foot | McCauslin's Farm |
| September 4 | McCauslin's Farm <br> waiting for Indian <br> guides and fair <br> weather | | |
| September 5 | McCauslin's Farm | bateau | North Twin Lake |
| September 6 | North Twin Lake | bateau | Abol Stream mouth |
| September 7 | Abol Stream | foot | Katahdin, near 3,800 ft. |
| September 8 | Katahdin <br> Abol Stream | foot <br> bateau | Abol Stream <br> Oak Hall Carry |
| September 9 | Oak Hall Carry <br> Quakish Lake | bateau <br> foot | **Quakish Lake** <br> **McCauslin's Farm** |
| September 10 | McCauslin's Farm <br> Medway <br> Mattawamkeag | foot <br> bateau <br> horse & buggy | Medway, 3½ miles <br> below Mattawamkeag <br> Bangor |
| September 11 | Bangor | steamer | Boston |

Maine historian Fannie Hardy Eckstorm found Thoreau a naturalist manqué. His ornithology was particularly lacking. Of the forty birds he saw in 1857, Eckstorm believed that seven were mistakes; three of these Thoreau himself questioned. Anyone who has tried seriously to learn birds while canoeing down river—especially without the aid of field guides and binoculars—as Thoreau was traveling, can appreciate the difficulty of the task. Furthermore, Thoreau did not kill birds, then the accepted method of positive identification employed by Audubon, Brewster, and Eckstorm's father, Manly Hardy.

*. . . wilderness . . . is . . . the raw material of all our civilization. (155)*

Thoreau also wanted to explore Maine, because it was a wilderness. This desire dictated his direction. His party approached Katahdin by the West Branch of the Penobscot River

**Thoreau's Chesuncook Trip, 1853, with George A. Thatcher and Joe Aitteon**

| Date | From | Via | To |
|---|---|---|---|
| September 13, Tuesday | Concord, Mass. Boston | train steamer | Boston somewhere along New England coast |
| September 14 | New England coast | steamer | Bangor, Maine |
| September 15 | Bangor | open wagon | Monson |
| September 16 | Monson Greenville Northeast Carry | open wagon steamer canoe | Greenville Northeast Carry Warren Island |
| September 17 | Warren Island | canoe | Pine Stream |
| September 18 | Pine Stream | canoe | Chesuncook Lake, Ansel Smith's |
| September 19 | Chesuncook Lake | canoe | Northeast Carry, north end |
| September 20 | Northeast Carry Greenville | steamer open wagon | Greenville Monson |
| September 21 | Monson | open wagon | Bangor |
| September 22 | Bangor Old Town | open wagon open wagon | Old Town Bangor |
| September 23 | Bangor | foot | Bangor |
| September 24 | Bangor | foot | Bangor |
| September 25 | Bangor | foot | Bangor |
| September 26 | Bangor | steamer | New England coast |
| September 27 | New England coast Boston | steamer train | Boston Concord |

in order to be immersed in virgin territory. Instead of descending the St. John River, they chose the East Branch because it passed through "the wildest country." (233)

Wilderness was an important focus of his thinking and writing. The word or its variants—wild, wilderness, wildly—recurs over one hundred times in *The Maine Woods*.[7] He rec-

**Thoreau's Allagash and East Branch Trip, 1857, with Edward S. Hoar and Joseph Polis**

| Date | From | Via | To |
|---|---|---|---|
| July 20, Monday | Concord, Mass.<br>Boston<br>Portland | train<br>train<br>steamer | Boston<br>Portland, Maine<br>Maine coast |
| July 21 | Maine coast | steamer | Bangor |
| July 22 | Bangor<br>Old Town<br>Indian Island | wagon<br>bateau<br>bateau, wagon | Old Town<br>Indian Island<br>Bangor |
| July 23 | Bangor | stage | Greenville |
| July 24 | Greenville | canoe | Kineo Peninsula |
| July 25 | Kineo Peninsula | canoe | West Branch |
| July 26 | West Branch | canoe | Caucomgomoc Stream |
| July 27 | Caucomgomoc Stream | canoe | Chamberlain Lake |
| July 28 | Chamberlain Lake | canoe | Chamberlain Farm |
| July 29 | Chamberlain Farm | canoe | Webster Brook, Grand Pitch |
| July 30 | Webster Brook | canoe | East Branch |
| July 31 | East Branch | canoe | East Branch, near Hunt's Farm |
| August 1 | East Branch | canoe | Penobscot River, below Medway |
| August 2 | Penobscot River | canoe | Chester, near Lincoln |
| August 3 | Chester<br>Old Town | canoe<br>train | Old Town<br>Bangor |
| August 4 | Bangor<br>Pushaw Lake | wagon<br>wagon | Pushaw Lake<br>Bangor |
| August 5 | Bangor<br>Old Fort Hill | wagon<br>wagon | Old Fort Hill<br>Bangor |
| August 6 | Bangor<br>Bucksport | wagon<br>wagon | near Bucksport<br>Bangor |
| August 7 | Bangor<br>Portland | train<br>steamer | Portland<br>Boston |
| August 8 | Boston | train | Concord |

ognized the virtues and limitations of wilderness. No matter how vast and powerful, it was still fragile and vulnerable. Protection, therefore, was a necessity, especially protection from man, who influenced it "as no other creature does." (151) Despite his need for wilderness, Thoreau realized that he could not live there; a "partially cultivated" landscape was his domicile. (155) That soil alone could nurture the fruits of humanity, its art, poetry, and music.

## ANTHROPOLOGICAL JOURNEY

> *Nature must have made a thousand revelations to them which are still secrets to us. (181)*

Indians deepened Thoreau's understanding of his environment. Native Americans interpreted North America for him. They lived in harmony with the earth, closer to its pulse. They had compassion for all living things. In Massachusetts, Thoreau visited with Indians, studied them, and collected their artifacts. In Maine, he came to know them intimately and of them he produced revealing portraits.

> *. . . for we had employed an Indian mainly that I might have an opportunity to study his ways. (95)*

Paddling with the Penobscots, Thoreau scrutinized their behavior. He made a reciprocal pact with Joe Polis that each would tell the other all he knew—and within eleven days! Thoreau was intrigued by the Penobscot language, and wanted to be a resident student on Indian Island. Indian materials fascinated him: "I made a faithful study of canoe-building, and I thought that I should like to serve an apprenticeship at that trade. . . ." (149) And, their uses of plants for food, drink, and medicine delighted him: "Our Indian said that he was a doctor, and could tell me some medicinal use for every plant I could show him. I immediately tried him." (235)

*George A. Thatcher*

Courtesy of James B. Vickery

## PSYCHOLOGICAL JOURNEY

This peripatetic also had another purpose. To know himself and his relationship to the universe was a paramount concern. Travel was a royal road to self-discovery. Like John Muir, Thoreau believed that going outside was really going inside one's self. And, he would have agreed with Dag Hammarskjöld, who later wrote that

> *The longest journey*
> *Is the journey inwards.*[8]

Part of the charm of *The Maine Woods* lies in the revelation of Thoreau's own character. His diverse personality is writ large, page after page. A few illustrations will suffice.

*A segment of* Coffin's Map of Massachusetts and Maine *that was used by Thoreau*

Thoreau was precise. He measured everything: distances between two points, moose, trees, ax handles, and tents. His exactness enables us to know what he saw and where he went, though his mileage is not always accurate.

Thoreau was also hale and hearty. After repeating his Maine trips, I have a greater respect for his physical strength. This was no effete soul who in his thirties paddled the length of Moosehead Lake, carried a sixty-pound pack for five miles between Umbazooksus and Chamberlain lakes, and led the ascent of Katahdin through trailless woods by compass.

He also had a sense of humor. It is evident that he had a lot of fun in Maine. He laughed at himself and at others. Banter between Polis and Thoreau continued day and night. Their peals of laughter resounding across the lakes must have cheered even the loons.

## JUDICIOUS JOURNEY

Many places could have met Thoreau's personal criteria for travel. Practical concerns also influenced his decision. His relatives, George and Rebecca Thatcher, lived in Bangor, Maine.[9] They greatly facilitated his vacations. He stayed at their home each time he entered and left the woods. George acted as his travel agent, making arrangements for gear, guides, and transportation. In 1846, he led Thoreau up the Penobscot River; in 1853, he accompanied him and their escort Joe Aitteon,[10] whose services he had obtained; and, in 1857, he introduced Thoreau to Joe Polis, whom he had known since he was a child. Without the Thatchers, Thoreau's wilderness experiences would not have been so pleasant and meaningful.

Bangor held other attractions as well. A growing community—it had become a city in 1834—it was filled with prosperity, excitement, and confidence. Geographically, it was ideally situated at the entrance of Maine's largest river, the Penobscot, and it was near to the Penobscot Indian village at Old Town. It was also accessible by public transportation. Thoreau could board a steamship in Boston and be in Bangor in less than twenty-four hours. By 1855, Boston and Bangor were joined by railroad; Thoreau traveled by rail to Portland from these cities on his last trips.

Each time I went to the Maine woods, I asked myself why I was there. Such reflection enabled me to touch the essence of the experience. Though many of my reasons were similar to Thoreau's, some were different. We did share a basic discovery: that is, that there is no limit to the satisfactions—emotional, physical, sensory, and intellectual—that can be derived from the Maine woods. Thus, we both kept coming back for more.

*You paddle along in a narrow canal through an endless forest, and the vision I have in my mind's eye, still, is of the small dark and sharp tops of tall fir and spruce trees, and pagoda-like* arbor-vitaes, *crowded together on each side, with various hard woods intermixed. (108)*

CHAPTER 2
# Moosehead Lake

The Indians called Moosehead Lake *Mspame,* "large water." There is, in fact, no bigger lake in New England: "twelve miles wide at the widest place, and thirty miles long in a direct line," Thoreau accurately measured, "but longer as it lies." (165) Two giant islands, together covering twelve square miles, do not begin to fill the lake's southern portion. A mountain rises like a mastodon from the lake's center. Your vision travels twelve miles without obstruction across North Bay. Forest encloses the lake. It runs from the shore in all directions, over hills and down valleys, interrupted only by rocky summits and wetlands. Spruce and fir, cedar, birches, maples, and aspens predominate. In summer, my impression is of an unlimited expanse of evergreens. Autumn beautifully contradicts. Deciduous trees also mantle this land; huge scarfs of red, brown, and yellow surround verdant shoulders.

To gain instant awareness of Moosehead's magnitude, climb Squaw Mountain (3,196 feet), five miles north of Greenville on Highway 6 and 15. A 3.25-mile trail leads to the summit.

## Greenville

On July 23, 1857, the Bangor stage pulled into Greenville, having made the seventy-mile trip the same day. The coach stopped at the inn of Joshua Fogg to discharge its passengers into the rain. One of them was a short and slender man of forty with a weathered face, brown hair, grayish-blue eyes, and an assortment of paraphernalia with which to sustain him in the North Woods for the next eleven days. (See his recommended "Outfit for an Excursion" —318–320.) He was Henry Thoreau of Concord, Mass., returning to Green- ville after a four-year absence. Accompanied by a friend, Edward Hoar, also of Concord, and a Penobscot Indian, Joe Polis, of Old Town, Maine, he entered the hotel for the night.[1] The next morning at four, they launched their birchbark canoe on Moosehead Lake.

James Russell Lowell's description of Greenville as "a little village which looks as if it had dripped down from the hills, and settled in the hollow at the foot of the lake" still fitted exactly the first time I saw the town, on July 28, 1974, at 6 p.m. Everything was dripping from the rain, which had recently halted. The sky appeared to be falling. It was too late and too wet for us to go to

*. . . a suitably wild looking sheet of water, sprinkled with small low islands, which were covered with shaggy spruce and other wild wood; . . . with mountains on each side and far in the north. (89)*

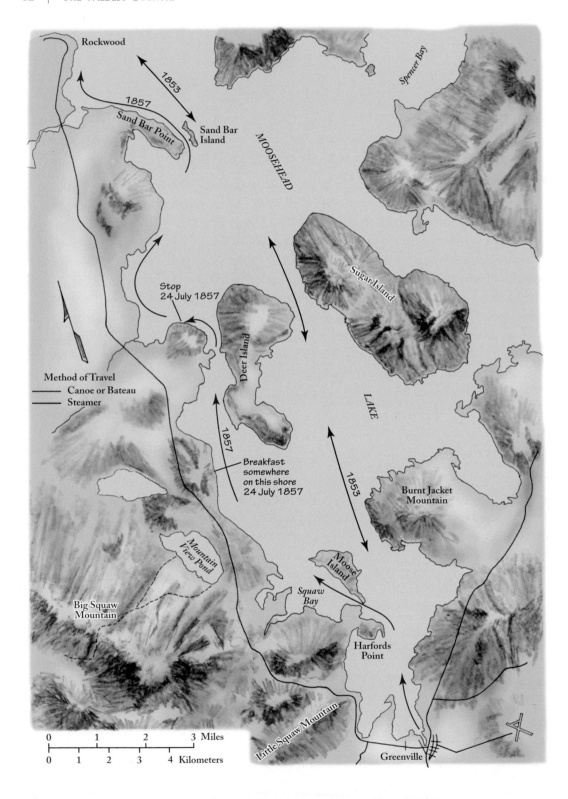

Rockwood

1853

1857

Sand Bar Point

Sand Bar
Island

MOOSEHEAD

Spencer Bay

Sugar Island

Stop
24 July 1857

Deer Island

Method of Travel
——— Canoe or Bateau
——— Steamer

LAKE

1857

Breakfast
somewhere
on this shore
24 July 1857

1853

Burnt Jacket
Mountain

Mountain
View Pond

Big Squaw
Mountain

Moose
Island

Squaw
Bay

Harfords
Point

Little Squaw Mountain

Greenville

| 0 | 1 | 2 | 3 Miles |

| 0 | 1 | 2 | 3 | 4 Kilometers |

Moose Island to camp. Joshua Fogg's tavern was not available, either. The Northeast Bank of Guilford had taken its place. The nearest campground was five miles away at Squaw Brook. In this damp clearing provided by Scott Paper Company we unrolled our tents.

For over a century Greenville has served the needs of Maine woods itinerants. Its hospitality is a tradition still upheld in many ways. A large signboard on Pritham Avenue, one block west of Main, displays a map of Thoreau's 1857 junket on Moosehead Lake. Local Indian artifacts are exhibited at the Moosehead Historical Society. At Shaw Public Library, you can read *Hubbard's Guide to Moosehead Lake,* a rare old book that is still relevant. Camping information and fire permits can be obtained from the district office of the Maine Forest Service (MFS) on Lakeview Street. Northwoods Outfitters on North Main offers everything for the outdoor enthusiast—U.S. Geological Survey maps, canoes, paddles, fishing licenses, and wool shirts.[2] In the past, a float plane could be chartered from an operator on the lake. When I visited Greenville in 1974, I asked the owner, Dick Folsom, who had been in business since 1946, what was the farthest distance his company had transported anyone from Greenville.

"Alaska," he replied.

"Besides there?"

"Ungava Bay," he said, referring to a spot which is north of the Labrador Peninsula.

"Are you the largest seaplane service in New England?" I queried, since that is what his literature claimed.

*The original Kineo House at Mount Kineo on Moosehead Lake*

Courtesy of the Maine Historic Preservation Commission

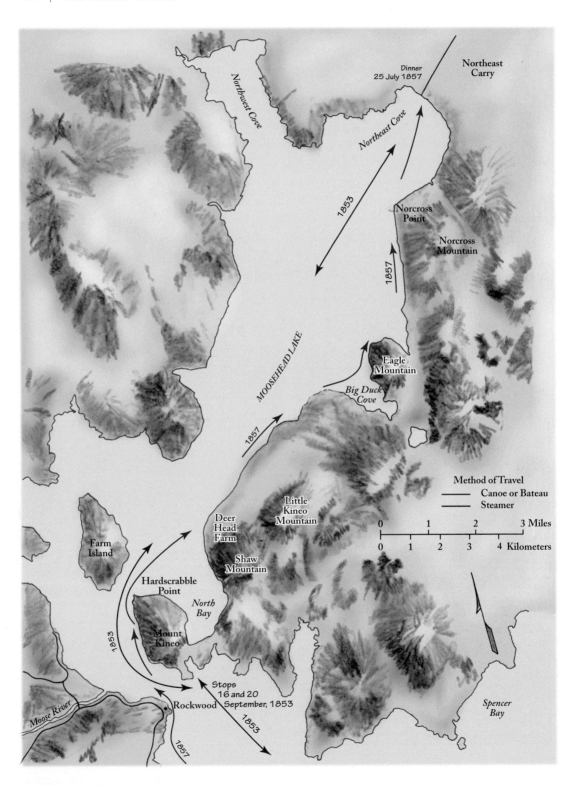

Northwest Cove

Dinner
25 July 1857

Northeast
Carry

Northeast Cove

1853

Norcross
Point

Norcross
Mountain

1857

MOOSEHEAD LAKE

Eagle
Mountain

Big Duck
Cove

1857

Method of Travel

Canoe or Bateau

Steamer

Little
Kineo
Mountain

Farm
Island

Deer
Head
Farm

Shaw
Mountain

0        1        2        3 Miles

0    1    2    3    4 Kilometers

Hardscrabble
Point

North
Bay

1853

Mount
Kineo

Stops
16 and 20
September, 1853

Moose River

Rockwood

1853

1857

Spencer
Bay

"Don't know anybody bigger," Folsom flatly stated. Then he added, "Rather be smaller sometimes."

Folsom's Air Service is now closed. Dick Folsom died in 2002, at age eighty-three. His son Max still flies and his other son, Rodney, still owns the lakefront property. You can visit Thoreau Park on the waterfront and purchase a map of the Thoreau-Wabanaki Trail at the Moosehead Marine Museum or Northwoods Outfitters.

*The Indian reminding us that he could not work without eating, we stopped to breakfast on the main shore, southwest of Deer Island, at a spot where* Mimulus ringens *grew abundantly. (166)*

## Greenville to Mount Kineo, 17.5 Miles

*We who had felt strangely as stage-passengers and tavern-lodgers were suddenly naturalized there and presented with the freedom of the lakes and the woods. (165)*

The modern canoeist can easily retrace Thoreau's 1857 route on Moosehead Lake.[3] Leaving Greenville, he went along the lake's east side for three miles, then "inclined to the western shore for the sake of its lee," passing between Harfords Point and Moose Island. Buoys now mark this navigable channel.

*Monkey flower*

### MOOSE ISLAND

In the late nineteenth century, John Cusac owned a large farm on Moose Island. Today, no vestiges of agriculture remain. Although the island is densely wooded and has no habitations, there are two campsites. On the eastern end is Poverty Point, whose ledges invite swimming and sunning. Should this small place be full, move on to a larger area at the island's north end.

### SQUAW POINT

After a breakfast consumed somewhere on the lake's western shore, Thoreau's party headed directly north between Deer Island and the mainland. Inspecting Squaw Point, the naturalist was rewarded with beaked hazelnut—"the only hazel which I saw on this journey"—bush honeysuckle, red osier dogwood, and rue taller than he was.[4] (170)

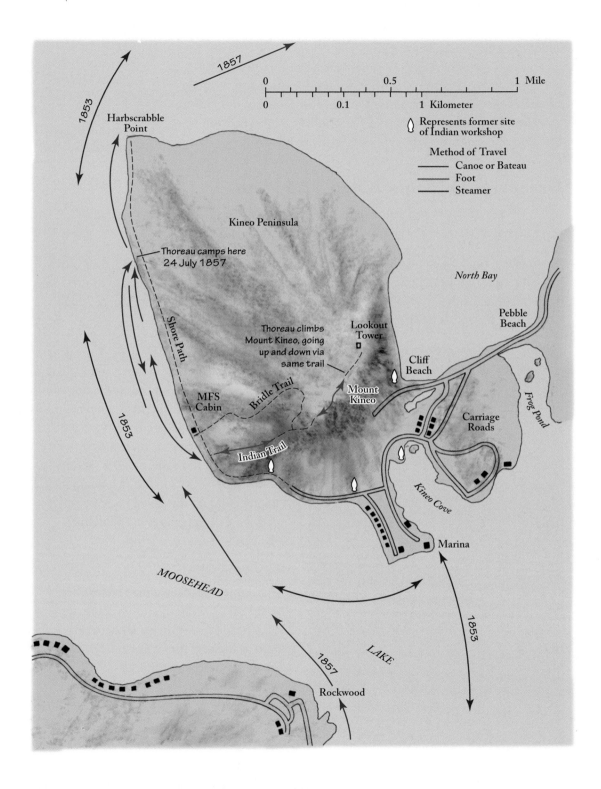

1857

1853

Harbscrabble
Point

0     0.5     1 Mile
0          0.1        1 Kilometer

⚲ Represents former site
of Indian workshop

Method of Travel
⎯⎯⎯ Canoe or Bateau
⎯⎯⎯ Foot
⎯⎯⎯ Steamer

Kineo Peninsula

North Bay

Thoreau camps here
24 July 1857

Pebble
Beach

Shore Path

Thoreau climbs
Mount Kineo, going
up and down via
same trail

Lookout
Tower

Cliff
Beach

Mount
Kineo

Frog Pond

MFS
Cabin

Bridle Trail

Carriage
Roads

1853

Indian Trail

Kineo Cove

Marina

MOOSEHEAD

1853

LAKE

1857

Rockwood

*Mountain cinquefoil*

## SAND BAR POINT AND ISLAND

After passing the East Outlet of the Kennebec River, they proceeded to Sand Bar Point where Thoreau and Polis "took the canoe over the bar, at Sand-bar Island, a few feet wide only, and so saved a considerable distance." (170) This carry is no longer necessary, since modern dams maintain a higher water level on Moosehead than the dam of Thoreau's day did.[5] I have regularly paddled between the point and the island—stopping on the point for a swim, of course. Sand Bar Island was purchased by Dr. Lee Salk, the prominent child psychologist, in 1969, "because it was very beautiful," he said.

On July 2, 1991, I visited Lee. He was having lunch when I arrived. Tomato juice and soup reached his intestines through a rubber tube. Cancer had forced the removal of his stomach and esophagus. He had not been able to work for a year. This afternoon, though, he intended to begin writing about his recovery.

"There were some funny parts to it," he smiled. Mary, his wife, was in Bangor, shopping in preparation for a visit from Lee's brother, Jonas Salk—the famous developer of the polio vaccine—and his wife. Also expected on the island that summer were Lee's son, Eric, a senior at Cornell Medical School, and his daughter, Pia, whose graduation from his alma mater, the University of Michigan, Lee had attended on May 4.

*The plants which chiefly attracted our attention on this mountain were the mountain cinquefoil (Potentilla tridentata), abundant and in bloom still at the very base, by the water-side, though it is usually confined to the summits of mountains in our latitude; very beautiful harebells overhanging the precipice; and bearberry . . . (176–177)*

CritterZone

*Bearberry*

That was the last time I saw Lee Salk. Two months later, on September 9, I stopped again, but he had left four days earlier, the caretaker told me. On May 2, 1992, Lee died. The family sold the island. His love of this island and Moosehead Lake and his vital spirit continue to inspire me.

The next landmark that Thoreau mentioned passing was "a broad bay opposite the mouth of Moose River, before reaching the narrow strait at Mount Kineo." (170–171) Actually, he was mistaken. He meant the mouth of the West Outlet of the Kennebec River; the Moose River lies north of Rockwood Point, which he had not yet attained. Thoreau's error is understandable when the map he was using is consulted (see Coffin's map of Maine, page 8).

The shortest passage across Moosehead Lake—⅝ mile—is between Rockwood and the Kineo Peninsula. Here Thoreau traversed the lake, coming "partly under the lee of the mountain, about a mile north of the Kineo House." (172) The party progressed half a mile farther north before making camp beneath the "dense spruce and fir wood on the side of the mountain." (173)

Hardscrabble Point, an ample campsite with generous views of Moosehead's North Bay, is one-half mile north of where Thoreau stayed; it is recommended for your night's lodging.

## KINEO PENINSULA

### *Thoreau's Journey*

> . . . *Mount Kineo is the principal feature of the lake.* . . . *(91)*

Thoreau climbed Mount Kineo on Friday, July 24, 1857, the same day he arrived at the peninsula. After preparing camp, his group returned southward along the shore by canoe to a small point. Here Thoreau and Hoar disembarked "and began to ascend the mountain along the edge of the precipice." (174) Their route approximated that of the present Indian Trail, which today is marked with blue paint. However, the trailhead isn't clearly marked.

Although Thoreau did not refer to a path, one existed. Twenty years earlier, on July 17, 1837, geologist James T. Hodge used Indian Trail to explore Mount Kineo. He noted that "the northern and western sides are covered with trees, and slope, so that one can reach the top by a path along the edge of the precipice."[6]

Like Hodge, Thoreau and Hoar followed the trail to the southeast end of the mountain, where they looked down "five or six hundred feet" into the water. Thoreau found this face of Kineo to be "its most remarkable feature." (176) He quoted geologist Charles T. Jackson's estimate of its height from the lake's surface, seven hundred feet.[7] After botanizing, they returned to the shore via the same route and paddled back to their campsite.

### *Kineo House*

Thoreau never stayed at Kineo House. In 1853, he made two stops at its landing, but he did not record his impressions of the place. There it stood before him, a small hotel which had served lumbermen, hunters, and tourists like himself for the last five years. The proprietor of the Greenville inn where Thoreau lodged, Joshua Fogg, built Kineo House in 1848 to accommodate the increasing number of travelers whose lake passage was booked on the steamer *Amphitrite*. The next year, 1849, a larger and faster steamer, *Moosehead,* began summer excursions from Greenville to Northeast Carry twice a week, stopping at the Kineo House each way. Thoreau first reached the Kineo peninsula on its decks.

A month earlier than Thoreau's visit, James Russell Lowell took the *Moosehead* to Kineo House. Unlike Thoreau, however, he unpacked his bags and stayed five days. Lowell approved of the congenial atmosphere, largely attributable to his jovial landlord, Harrison G. O. Barrows, who "with a voice as clear and strong as a northwest wind, and a great laugh suitable to it" waited upon his "neat and well supplied" table. He also liked the cost: three dollars per day. A typical guest, Lowell hired guides, camped in the woods, hunted moose, fished, and climbed Mount Kineo. Later he related his vacation in an entertaining tale (see Further Reading and the Afterword).

*The second Kineo House*

Courtesy of Special Collections, Raymond H. Fogler Library, University of Maine at Orono

The Kineo House which Fogg established burned in 1868—an historic landmark gone. Another, larger hotel, also destroyed by fire, was followed by a third, opening in the summer of 1884 and featuring electric bells, steam heat, elevators, bathrooms, a telegraph, post office, billiard halls, a 400-seat dining room, orchestra performances, and modern fire escapes—all this in the middle of the Maine woods. Neither Thoreau nor Lowell could have envisioned such a future. Finally, in the early twentieth century, the hotel was transformed into a complete resort community with horses and carriages, golf, and sailing. The hotel was a megalosaur unable to sustain itself and was demolished in 1938.

Although the resort did not last, you can still stay on the Kineo peninsula where so many of the nineteenth century vacationers did. From June through October, the Oak Lodge (opened in 1912), in the center of a row of privately-owned cottages along the west shore, is available for rental. This is now an historic district, Oak Lodge's Karen Musser told me. She recommended reading Durward Ferland's *Kineo Splendor and Silence.* Another accommodation is the brand new Kineo House (opened in 2006), secluded in the woods at the base of the mountain by a pond near the nine-hole golf course. "It's actually between two fairways," the owner, Jim Mitchell, said, "but you can't see either one from the house."

## Tours

Kineo is most easily reached today from Rockwood, less than a mile due west across the lake. Rockwood, twenty miles north of Greenville on Highway 6 and 15, offers campgrounds, motels, general stores, and boat services.

**Shore Path: Hardscrabble Point to Kineo Coves**

| Southbound Cumulative Mileage | Features | Description |
|:---:|---|---|
| .00 | Hardscrabble Point | Camping, swimming, and fishing are possible here. |
| .50 | Thoreau's Camp, July 24, 1857 | He camped in the woods about 96 feet from the shore. |
| 1.25 | MFS Cabin Bridle Trail | Bridle Trail starts behind this cabin; it climbs gradually through the woods until joining Indian Trail in .75 mi. The trail then proceeds .5 mi. to the summit, where an abandoned MFS fire tower offers views of the country. Return to the Bridle Trail to Maine Forest Service (MFS) cabin or take Indian Trail, which departs (left) from Bridle Trail .5 mi. from summit, descending along south face of the mountain 3.8 mi. to Shore Path. |
| 1.37 | Indian Trail | This trail, marked with blue paint, leaves Shore Path, ascending steeply along the southwest precipice until a clearing is reached from which the southern portion of Kineo Peninsula and Moosehead Lake can be seen. Your eye scans Thoreau's course up Moosehead, backward to Sand Bar, Deer, and Moose islands. Beyond this lookout the trail enters the woods to join the Bridle Trail, which proceeds .5 mi. to the MFS tower on the summit. |
| 1.62 | Indian Workshop | For a discussion of these workshops, see "Maine Woods Landforms" at the end of this chapter. |
| 2.00 | Indian Workshop | |
| 2.50 | Kineo Cove | Boat service is provided between here and Rockwood. |

*The third Kineo House in 1896*

Kineo is a pleasant place to visit for an afternoon, or for a week or more. There is plenty to see and do. I have enjoyed the following tours. Modify them as you wish.

### Shore Path Walking Tour, 5 Miles Round Trip

A path along the western edge of the peninsula joins Hardscrabble Point in the north with Kineo Cove in the south. This path can be taken in either direction, partially or entirely, with an optional side trip up the mountain. The former sites of Thoreau's camp and Indian workshops are passed. The guide on page 21 indicates the places of interest and the approximate distances between them. If you begin at Kineo Cove, merely reverse the table.

### Pebble and Cliff Beaches Walking Tours, 2.5 Miles Round Trip

After arriving at Kineo Cove, you may wish to explore the east side of the peninsula. From the marina, proceed northward along the west shore of Kineo Cove to its northwest corner, where another ancient Indian workshop was located. A carriage path, marked as private property, leads to the right. Kineo Hotel guests in horse-drawn carriages drove over this road to Deer Head Farm on the mainland for an excursion. To reach Pebble and Cliff beaches, follow the carriage road to the left (west) past the golf course shop to a fairway where a golf course road leads north. Follow this road north and then back east along the forest at the base of the great cliff, reaching the North Bay at Cliff Beach. Pebble Beach is farther along the lake shore to the east.

Standing at Cliff Beach, I looked up at the southeast face of Mount Kineo, wondering if anyone had scaled this craggy surface. Another Indian workshop was situated at the west end of the beach. The return route is along your outward path.

### Canoeing Tour, 6.5 Miles Round Trip

Paddling around the Kineo peninsula presents a different perspective from the one gained by strolling over its landscape. By making the appropriate stops, all of the places on the above walking tours can be seen as well. There is a short carry over the isthmus at Pebble Beach, which provides a convenient place for lunch. Incidentally, crossing the isthmus is the shortest way from the southern end of the lake to North Bay or vice versa; the boater saves two miles by not rounding Hardscrabble Point.

## Mount Kineo to Northeast Carry, 14 Miles

From Mount Kineo, Thoreau embarked to complete the paddling of Moosehead Lake. Fourteen miles remained. His course followed the eastern side of the lake. Crossing the bay between Hardscrabble Point and Deer Head Farm, he headed northward along the shore to Norcross Point, from which he went across Northeast Cove to the landing.

When calm, the North Bay of Moosehead is a delightful trip of four hours. Your voyage need not be hastened to assure yourself a place for the night, for the east side of the lake offers three campgrounds at the luxurious Big Duck Cove. Except for the campsites and a few houses, the lakeshore is forested. Spruce, fir, arbor vitae, and birch abound. These trees run from the lake over the tops of adjacent mountains: Norcross, Eagle, Shaw. The only exposed summit is that of Little Kineo, which is higher than Kineo.

### NORTHEAST CARRY

The boundary between Moosehead and the Penobscot is not spectacular. Somehow you expect more when passing between Maine's largest lake and river. Instead, the divide is almost imperceptible, the topography flat. From the lake, the terrain rises slightly—fifty-eight feet to be exact—to the midpoint, then inclines gently in the other direction, downward more than one hundred feet to the river. On the north side, surface water travels into the West Branch of the Penobscot River, which meets the Penobscot before it flows into the Atlantic Ocean. South of the divide, the flow runs to the sea via Moosehead Lake and the Kennebec River. Both ways to the Gulf of Maine are the same distance, 188 miles.

People have been crossing this height of land for centuries. An Indian trail provided the first connection. In the nineteenth century, the state built a road, which James T. Hodge, using it in July 1837, found to be "out of repair, muddy, and encumbered by fallen trees and bushes."[8] Improvement of this approach coincided with the harvesting of timber on the

West Branch. In 1842, a tramway was built to transport supplies to lumberers. Eleven years later, Thoreau employed this "rude log railway" to haul his baggage through the woods. (93)

In August 1856, a distinguished duo reached Northeast Carry by steamer from Greenville. They were author Theodore Winthrop and artist Frederic Edwin Church. They journeyed the length of the Penobscot to Old Town, climbing Mount Katahdin on the way. Winthrop wrote an account of their trip, *Life in the Open Air,* which was published in 1863, the year before *The Maine Woods* appeared (see Afterword and Further Reading for Chapter Nine). In his book Winthrop characterized the Northeast Carry:

> *A wharf promised a settlement, which, however, did not exist. There was population, —one man and one great ox. Following the inland-pointing nose of the ox, we saw, penetrating the forest, a wooden railroad. Ox-locomotive, and no other, befitted such trails. The train was one great go-cart. We packed our traps upon it, roofed them with our birch, and, without ceremony of whistling, moved on.*

*Mount Kineo*

Thoreau enjoyed his walk across Northeast Carry. A profusion of wildflowers enter-
Thoreau enjoyed this walk across the Northeast Carry. A profusion of wildflowers entertained him. The clearing for the railway provided light for their growth. (Spruces and firs
shut out sunlight; few plants can survive in their shade.) Heaths grew abundantly—pale
laurel, Labrador tea, Canada blueberry, creeping snowberry—as did lily family members—
clintonia, large-flowered bellwort, and painted trillium. The honeysuckles were represented
by twinflower. Yellow goldenrod, red trumpet weed, and the pale violet rays of rough-
leaved aster were also in bloom that late summer day.

These flowers, the surrounding forest, and the railroad were destroyed. They all went
up in flames, the landscape bared and blackened. What you see today is new growth of
the last century.[9]

Scenes at both ends of the Carry differ from what Thoreau witnessed, too. On the
lakeside, the steamboat wharf is gone. The wilderness "where not a cabin nor a mortal
was to be seen" had been opened for the Northeast Carry Inn, which for years offered
wayfarers meals, lodging, and drayage service. (92–93) Though closed to the public, the
establishment still stands. On the West Branch, Thoreau found a sixty-acre clearing with
storehouse, lumberer's quarters, and Samuel Hinckley's home. Nearby three Indians were
settled temporarily; he joined them for the night.[10] Today cars park beside the river and
buildings are located where Thoreau slept.

When I was there, on August 4, 1987, with Thoreau scholar Ronald Wesley Hoag
and his friend Dana S. Brigham, two counselors and six campers from the all-boys camp,
Flying Moose Lodge, came ashore in four wood-canvas canoes. Having paddled from
Greenville in two days, camping at Deer Island and Seboomook Point, they carried
food for two weeks, enough to reach Fort Kent on the St. John River. In a *Boston Globe*
op-ed piece published in late 2006, the former executive director of the Appalachian
Trail Conference, Larry Van Meter, lamented that primitive camps such as Flying Moose
Lodge are now rare.

About forty minutes is required to walk the two miles between Moosehead Lake
and the West Branch. Follow Northeast Carry Road straight across. Make no turns. In
three-quarters of a mile another road departs right for the cottages on Northeast Cove.
One-half mile before the river, the Seboomook Lake Road intersects. Approximately two
hundred yards from the river on the west side is a good spring. You can drive your car to
the West Branch and start your canoe trip there, if you wish.

---

# Maine Woods Landforms

## Mount Kineo

With the exception of the resort, the rest of the Kineo peninsula looks natural. The landscape, though constantly changing, appears now about as it did to Thoreau and to countless generations of Indians who came here before him. The first visitors were prehistoric Indians, called "red paint people" because they painted red ocher on their bodies and belongings, and even took it with them to their graves. One of their cemeteries was located near the Kineo Hotel; it was destroyed for the pleasure of playing tennis.

The central attraction of Kineo to these Indians and their successors, tribes of the eastern Abenaki, was its stone. Thoreau described the appearance of local stone in 1857 as

*... generally slate-colored, with white specks, becoming a uniform white where exposed to the light and air, and it breaks with a conchoidal fracture, producing a ragged cutting edge. (176)*

AMC Library and Archives

*A canoeist on Moosehead Lake in 1896*

His portrait is still accurate. Today you can see these colors and shapes in the stone.

What was it made of? "Hornstone, like flint," as the first Maine State Geologist, Charles T. Jackson, identified it in 1838. And, this was not just a small deposit, but the largest known in the world, according to him. (We are now aware of even greater accumulations.[11])

The composition of this stone was first analyzed by Professor Edward S. C. Smith in 1925. He concluded that it was a rhyolite, mostly made up of quartz and orthoclase, which is a feldspar. Dr. Arthur J. Boucot, who conducted the most extensive studies of the geology of this area in the 1940s and 1950s, agreed with Smith.

How old is it? About 375 million years, Dr. Boucot believed, dating from the late Lower Devonian period.

Indians came from all over Maine, if not from greater distances, for this ancient rhyolite. For them, Kineo was one of the richest sources of raw material in New England. Not all journeyed to Moosehead Lake; some of the Kineo rhyolite was carried southward by glacial ice, dispersing it in smaller pockets, which the Indians also used. The real treasure trove, however, was at the mountain.

Nature performed much of the work of shaping the stone for the Indians. Weathering caused erosion of the south face of Kineo. Slowly and continually, tons of rock broke off from the side of the mountain and fell to the ground below, forming a slope of fragments. The resulting precipice and talus can be seen today. These shattered pieces of rock were just what the Indians wanted for their tools and weapons. They did not have to mine them. They picked them up from the surface of the pile and brought them to the edges of the lake (to the workshops located on the map), not far from where they were found. There the Indians sorted them, roughly fashioning the desirable ones. Many resembled the shape of the final product in their natural state and needed little further effort. The Indians then took their collections to their villages on the Kennebec and Penobscot rivers, where they crafted the final designs. A scraper, arrowhead, or knife might emerge.[12]

Kineo rhyolite, then, entered the natives' homes and, in one form or another, became widely distributed. It traveled far beyond the borders of Maine. Jackson discovered it in all parts of New England. Thoreau also stated that he had "found hundreds of arrow-heads made of the same material." (176) Some of these he discovered on the shores of the Concord River in Massachusetts, where the Penobscots came to trade and camp.

*It was very exhilarating, and the perfection of travelling, quite unlike floating on our dead Concord River, the coasting down this inclined mirror, which was now and then gently winding, down a mountain, indeed, between two evergreen forests . . . (252)*

### CHAPTER 3

# West Branch of the Penobscot,
## Northern Section

### Northeast Carry to Chesuncook Lake, 20 Miles

Opposite Northeast Carry on the West Branch sits a small cabin nearly enveloped by forest. At one time this was the summer residence of Carl and Mona Mayhew of Gardiner, Maine. On the evening of August 4, 1975, Mrs. Mayhew introduced herself to me from across the river: "I watched you coming over the portage with your canoe; you didn't stop."

"Bugs wouldn't let me," I smiled. "There's a letter for you."

"For me?" She sounded surprised, as I was not her usual postman. In the Maine woods, however, anyone is liable to be a carrier. Customarily, nineteenth-century travelers conveyed mail to people living along their routes. This old tradition was perpetuated by the former proprietor of the Northeast Carry Inn, W. J. Lacrosse, who asked me to deliver Mrs. Mayhew's letter. "I'll come over," she said.

"Don't bother. I'll bring it." The nearest post office is Rockwood on Moosehead Lake, forty-five miles away on paper company roads. Steamers used to transport mail from Rockwood to the Northeast Carry. Since 1946, however, Clarence Johnston had been bringing it in his four-wheel-drive pickup every weekday. The trip takes an hour and a half. His destination is Lobster Stream, from whence he returns to Rockwood.[1]

"Have you seen anybody else today?" I mustered the courage to ask, anxious to know our chances of finding empty campsites.

"Sixty today," she exclaimed with resignation. "They all went downstream."

"Guess we'll stay right here tonight." I let my unhappiness show.

No fires permitted there, she warned.

There was no question about my mood now. "We'll eat cold beans."

"Worst place in the world for flies."

"We'll put up a tent."

I paddled her letter across the river, then went back over the carry two more times for our gear.

Entering the West Branch, the scene changes dramatically. Gone are the panoramic vistas of Moosehead. Gone are the mountains whose summits can be seen from any part

0    1    2    3    4   Miles

0   1   2   3   4   5   Kilometers

1857

1853

Chesuncook

Chesuncook Lake

Ansel Smith's Night
18 Sept. 1853

1853

Dinner
17 & 19 Sept.
1853

Big Island

Pine Stream

Camp
17 Sept. 1853

Ragmuff Stream

River

Thoreau travels to here, then returns to W. Br. Penobscot Joe Aitteon goes ½ mile further

Thoreau bathes in stream
26 July 1857

Smith Halfway House

1857

Penobscot

Beaver Brook

1853

West Branch

Moosehorn Stream

Salmon Pond

1853

Camp
25 July
1857

Camp–South of island
16 Sept. 1853

Thoreau fishes in mouth of stream
25 July 1857

1857

Camp
19 Sept.
1853

Northeast Carry

Lobster Stream

1853

Dinner
25 July
1857

Lobster Lake

1853

MOOSEHEAD LAKE

Ogden Point

Method of Travel

——— Canoe or Bateau

——— Foot

——— Steamer

*Canoeists on Sourdnahunk Stream. Thoreau mentions this waterway in* The Maine Woods *and raves about its fishing.*

of the lake. Gone are the expansive feelings generated by the sweep of mind and vision over miles of water and woods. In the Penobscot Valley, confinement prevails. "You paddle along in a narrow canal through an endless forest," Thoreau said of the river, between "the small dark and sharp tops of tall fir and spruce trees, and pagoda-like arbor-vitaes, crowded together on each side, with various hard woods intermixed." (108)

The West Branch begins twenty miles west of (and upstream from) Northeast Carry at Pittston Farm, where the North and South branches of the Penobscot converge. Its start is a deadwater, Seboomook Lake, created by a dam built in the mid-1890s. The lake's shape, two plump sausage links, gives away its riverine heritage. Below the dam, and about five miles upstream of Northeast Carry, the river contracts to its ancient channel, offering canoeists smooth and rapid water. From Northeast Carry downstream to Chesuncook Lake is a pleasant, unobstructed, twenty-mile paddle. From Chesuncook, the West Branch flows sixty-eight miles to Medway, where it meets the East Branch to form the Penobscot. The West Branch is longer than the Penobscot; it is the fifth longest river in Maine.

Thoreau became well acquainted with this territory. He descended the West Branch to Chesuncook Lake twice—in September 1853 and again in July 1857. On the former trip he returned upstream from Chesuncook to Northeast Carry. He spent three nights on the river. He searched its tributaries—Lobster, Moosehorn, Ragmuff, and Pine streams—for moose. He camped on the latter. You can do likewise.

## LOBSTER STREAM AND LAKE

Two and a half miles below Northeast Carry, a low, grassy islet marks the junction of Lobster Stream with the West Branch. Here the river turns north, while the stream enters from the south. A wooden bridge spans the stream's mouth; here cars park.

To get from the West Branch to Lobster Lake, you take Lobster Stream. This two-mile trip is clear and comfortable. The current, which is barely discernable, can go either way, as Thoreau noted. (97) Its normal flow is north, but when the West Branch rises above the lake's level, the water runs the other direction.

Thoreau missed Lobster Lake. He ascended Lobster Stream about a mile-and-a-half before returning mooseless. Had he gone a little farther, he would have absorbed the feeling of well-being that Lobster Lake engenders.

He might have relaxed on Ogden Point, for many years my favorite stopping place. Looking southward from this sandpit, you see surrounding hills and mountains. The highest, Big Spencer Mountain, sits solid and alone, seven miles distant. Its face is broad and forested; its head, flat—a two-mile plateau over 3,000 feet high. Its sides incline steeply at the top, then flare at the base. The sunrise at this spot on August 21, 1978, was a magical one, as I noted in my journal:

> *Cold morning. Silk veils of mist from the lake. Mergansers swimming. Light strikes the mountain first, coloring its green slate-gray. Hills beneath are black. Sky beyond, pure azure. A cloud rests on the pinnacle's west end, a white ribbon pausing on its passage in the wind.*

Sadly, Ogden Point is no longer open to the public. In 1979, the new owners of the land requested that the two Maine Forest Service (MFS) campsites be removed. Two other MFS facilities are available elsewhere: one on the west shore of Little Claw at a rock ledge; the other at the south end of Big Claw.

Lobster Lake has good fishing—or at least the Mainers tell me so. Two gentlemen from Bowdoin caught fifteen salmon in one week. "We lost a lot and threw some back," they added. The best place for salmon is between Ogden Point and Lobster Stream; for trout, look south of the point in the narrows.

In the nineteenth century, Lobster Lake had several names. Thoreau learned three of them.[2] One map he used—created by George W. Coffin in 1835—designated it *Matahumkeag*. Polis called it *Beskabekuk*. (189) And, Aitteon used its

*Canada lily*

present name to acknowledge the fresh water lobsters found there. (97) Of course, he was referring to crayfish of the genus *Cambarus* which live in fresh water, and not their larger, salt water cousins of the genus *Homarus,* which always come to mind when the lake is mentioned. Some also find the lake's form to resemble the shape of these crustaceans.

*Lobster Lake in 1900*

## MOOSEHORN STREAM

Two miles below Lobster Stream, you pass under a bridge for timber-hauling trucks. Just beyond lies Warren Island, with a campsite at its southern end where Thoreau stayed.

In three and a half miles, Moosehorn enters the West Branch. A short stream of three miles, it drains Salmon Pond Marsh to the south. Thoreau penetrated this waterway as far as Beaver Brook, one-half mile, before departing. He found no moose, only hay stacked along the shore, cut for lumber operations. (102) Today, speckled alders, *Alnus rugosa,* and thick tussocks of sedges, *Carex vesicaria,* line the shore and fill the channel.[3] The start of the stream can be canoed, but afterwards it becomes too narrow and overgrown to navigate.

## RAGMUFF STREAM

Ragmuff debouches into the West Branch two miles below Moosehorn Stream. Joe Polis called it *Paytaytequick,* meaning "burnt ground stream." (195) Every time Thoreau went by, he stopped—for dinner and fishing on September 17, 1853; for dinner, bathing, and botanizing on September 19, 1853; and for bathing on July 26, 1857. Aitteon walked two miles up Ragmuff—it goes seven—and spotted a moose, but being unarmed he made no kill.

This is still a popular place. A commodious campsite now resides on the point made by Ragmuff and the West Branch. Trout are caught in the stream. A path, leading from the camp, follows Ragmuff's east side. Walking is the best way to ascend its course, since there is a small falls near its mouth.

## PINE STREAM

From Ragmuff to Pine Stream is seven and a half miles. In two miles Big Island divides the West Branch, and the current increases. Many campsites surround the island.

*We soon after saw a splendid yellow lily (Lilium Canadense) by the shore, which I plucked. It was six feet high and had twelve flowers, in two whorls, forming a pyramid, such as I have seen in Concord . . . The Indian asked what we called it, and said that the "loots" (roots) were good for soup, that is, to cook with meat, to thicken it, taking the place of flour. (189)*

AMC Library and Archives

*White water below Sourdnahunk Falls in the 1930s*

As you paddle from Big Island to Pine Stream, imagine this entire section of the river filled with long logs—25 to 30 million feet of lumber—and not even a tub-full of open water to put your canoe in. This is exactly what happened in 1900, when wood jammed at Northeast Carry, remaining through the winter. In the spring, with a new harvest added to the old, two years' cuttings moved down the West Branch. Pine Stream Falls stopped everything. Five miles of liquid went solid. Men worked all summer to clear the entanglement. The logs did not reach Bangor until November 11. That day almost a foot of snow fell, enclosing the logs in the Penobscot River for the second winter.[4]

Pine Stream is the longest tributary between Northeast Carry and Chesuncook Lake. It runs south thirteen and a half miles from Big Pine Pond, near Ragged Lake. Polis knew Pine Stream as Black River, *Karsaootuk;* he had traveled it on his way south to Caribou Lake. (195)

Today you can retrace Thoreau's journey along Pine Stream. He went up about three and a half miles before returning. At the start the course is wide and clear. Not far from the mouth on the west side, George Thatcher wounded a moose. (110) The stream then meanders through a marsh. After an hour, the channel becomes too rocky and shallow to paddle. This is the place, I believe, where Thoreau portaged. (112) After the carry, where the moose shot earlier was found dead, the party was able to paddle for a mile. This is now impossible unless unusually high water prevails. It is easiest to advance afoot using the streambed.

Thoreau moved along the shore in "the worst of walking, a perfect chaos of fallen and drifted trees"—a portrayal still painfully accurate, as I discovered when I explored the route. I broke through dead branches, stepped over rotten logs, and sought open corridors. I knew that I could never portage my canoe through these wilds; there was even some question whether I could get myself through. Trudging along in the water is better than in the woods. Soon I met a rock ledge over which the stream drops half a foot or so. This location comes the closest to Thoreau's description of "a considerable fall" at whose foot he spent the night of September 17, 1853. (117) After dinner, they hunted up the stream for a mile farther, Aitteon going half a mile more. They returned to the falls for the night, leaving the next day for the West Branch.[5]

## PINE STREAM FALLS

In Thoreau's time an extensive stretch of white water, called Pine Stream Falls, churned up the West Branch below where Pine Stream enters. Thoreau portaged this cascade twice, while his Indian guides ran the canoes through. Two pitches provided a thrill. In her journal, Fannie Hardy Eckstorm recounted her ride of August 13, 1889, down this same stretch with her father Manly Hardy, and guide, Reed McPheters:

*Passengers in a bateau on the West Branch of the Penobscot*

> *We got down onto the head of Pine Stream [Falls] and ran on the right. In the worst place in the Upper Pitch, Reed caught his pole and lost it. The canoe broached to, caught and cracked heavily, coming near swamping. We ran through on a paddle and caught the pole, and then came part way down the Lower Pitch when father and I got out and left him to run it down.[6]*

The excitement of shooting Pine Stream Falls is gone. Chesuncook Dam, completed the winter of 1903–1904, put a stop to this fun. Assuming its new size, Chesuncook Lake spread over the West Branch, smoothing the rough surface of Pine Stream Falls and Rocky Rips, one mile above. Today the West Branch glides serenely by, unaware of its predecessor's turbulence.

Approaching Chesuncook Lake, the West Branch widens. Mud flats appear. On the shores, small shells, 2¾ inches long and 1¾ inches wide, are scattered or stacked in tiny, neat piles. Their black and brown halves are ajar, exposing a milky-white and purple opalescent interior. The inhabitants, flattened filter clams, *Elliptio complanata,* endemic to the eastern United States and Canada from the St. Lawrence River to the Gulf of Mexico, are missing, probably digested by muskrats or raccoons.[7] Later, my companions find more of these mussels in the shallows and cook them for dinner.

---

# Maine Woods Animals

**Eastern Moose,** *Alces alces americana*

*They made me think of great frightened rabbits, with their long ears and half inquisitive half frightened looks; the true denizens of the forest.... (110)*

Moose inhabit the boreal forest around the globe. The species prevalent in northern Maine, as well as in the surrounding Canadian provinces, is the eastern moose. In the summer, I have seen them along most of Thoreau's waterways—the Penobscot's West and East branches, Lobster and Pine streams, the Allagash, Webster Brook, and ponds in Baxter State Park.

A good place to observe moose is along rivers and lakes. At your coming, the timid lope up to the banks into the woods, surprisingly quickly and quietly for their size. They move, shy but not frightened, from the water to the first line of trees to await your departure. The brave do not budge. They hold their position even in the presence of *Homo sapiens*. On September 1, 1977, my canoe drifted within twenty feet of a cow, who was breakfasting on Allagash River plants, her head beneath the surface. I thought that we would pass by without her noticing, but she soon raised her

*Male eastern moose*

Jerry and Marcy Monkman/EcoPhotography

head. She stared stoically at us, chomping her well-washed greens through which water drained from her muzzle back into the river. Pausing long enough to decide that we were not worth the interruption of her repast, she went down for another mouthful. The following year in late August, a cow and her calf cropped the shallows of Russell Pond within one hundred yards of our lean-to. They ate until dark—for over three hours—not disturbed by sightseers, campers, photographers, and the constant rain.

Moose are liable to be anywhere, however, even on highways and mountains. In August 1978, I was hiking up North Traveler in Baxter State Park. At about 2,000 feet, a side trail leads to Ellsworth Spring, where I stopped for a drink. Kneeling while refreshing myself, I looked directly into two lugubrious eyes peering above the ferns at the edge of a birch grove. I stood up. A dark form rose from the shadows. I took five steps backward. A large bull came forward wearing fur-covered antlers with thirteen points. Was he searching for a place to rub off his velvet? I kept going in the opposite direction. He regarded my ungracious retreat from his charming company with a stolid expression, flopping his ears sympathetically and scratching his head and sides with his legs. Returning from the summit an hour and a half later, and with renewed courage, I went by to see if my friend was still there. Sure enough, he was, settled back down in the shade for his nap.

At such moments when moose are met face-to-face, it is reassuring to know their eating habits. They are herbivores, dining exclusively on plants. Their diet depends on the season. Their winter fare consists of twigs and branches of conifers and deciduous trees: balsam fir, red osier dogwood, quaking aspen, sweet viburnum, mountain ash, beaked hazelnut, and an assortment of willows, cherries, and birches. Moose also enjoy the barks of many of these trees, especially when the sap is rising.

In the spring, the menu changes. Conifers are abandoned in favor of fresh leaves, which they harvest en masse by sliding branches through their mouths. Defoliation is instant and complete. With warmer weather, they also shop for herbaceous and aquatic plants. The waterfront offers a mélange of nutrition. Their meal might include yellow pond lilies with water-shield and eel grass; or, lacking these, sweet-scented water lilies with bur-reeds and pond weeds for dessert. The ornithologists Helen and Allen Cruickshank watched a bull completely submerge himself while feeding in Sandy Stream Pond near Katahdin.[8] Captivated, they produced a film of the episode. Moose indulge in aquatic vegetation until it loses its flavor in late summer. Then it's back to the woods.

But they do not go for food alone. Moose have other needs to attend to now. Their breeding season begins about mid-September, and lasts one month. What better time to make love in the wilderness than in the splendor of autumn, and without the annoyance of bugs? In this period the appetite of the bull decreases. Eating little and traveling much in search of a mate, he loses weight, as much as 150 pounds, one authority estimates.[9] The cow, on the other hand, stays put and increases her girth. They find each other by calling: the male grunts; the female wails. Once together, intimacy develops through quieter conversations and play. One of their favorite games is to roll in a wallow, which the bull digs with his front hooves and wets with his waste.

The Indians took advantage of moose communication during the rut. By imitating the cow's call they were able to lure the male within gun range. (March 5, 1858) They inveigled the moose with a birchbark megaphone "about fifteen inches long and three or four wide at the mouth, tied round with strips of the same bark," which sounded to Thoreau like a great horned owl— "*ugh ugh ugh*, or *oo oo oo oo*." (101) While on the West Branch, Joe Aitteon made such a horn for their hunt, but he had no luck with it. Instead of their surprising a moose, the one they did kill stood so silently in Pine Stream that they nearly drifted by it.

For humans, moose often meant survival. The animals provided food, clothing, and money for the Abenaki, missionaries, and settlers of Maine. All parts of the moose were used. The body was butchered for meat, a staple of the Penobscots. Hunters cooked and ate the flesh to sustain them on their travels. Thoreau and his guides had such fare for breakfast and supper. (122, 129) The bulk, however, was preserved for later. Smoked or dried for three or four days, the meat could be kept a year. The heart, lip, tongue, and nose were also consumed, the latter being a delicacy. (132) Often, a moose leg flavored corn soup.

The coat of the moose furnished wearing apparel. A pair of mittens or socks could be woven from the thick gray wool of the underside of the mane; skins of hind legs were fashioned read-

ily into waterproof
for canoes, which c
1850) In the woods
a rack, a process Tl
processing, though
ceived $2.25 for his
as much in Old Tow

*For my dessert, I helped myself to a large slice of the Chesuncook woods,
and took a hearty draught of its waters with all my senses. (129)*

## CHAPTER 4
# Chesuncook Lake

The original Chesuncook—a shallow stream flowing amidst wide, grassy meadows and soft, loamy banks—is no more. A series of dams, built between 1840 and 1916, changed the river meadow into Maine's third largest lake.[1]

An Indian definition of Chesuncook—"a place where many streams emptied in"—accurately depicted the geography of the lake's northwest corner, where three tributaries converged: Penobscot's West Branch, Caucomgomoc, and Umbazooksus.[2] (141) Their meeting is less pronounced today than in the 1850s, when Thoreau traveled them, because Ripogenus Dam (1916) has flooded their mouths, changing the configuration of northern Chesuncook.

## Ansel Smith's

*I was interested to see how a pioneer lived on this side of the country. (124)*

In September 1853, Thoreau went from the West Branch down the west shore of Chesuncook Lake to the first clearing, the property of Ansel Smith (1849).[3] Here he spent the night. Smith's land, extending "two miles down the lake by half a mile in width," comprised forest and meadow. Within a hundred-acre field stood his vegetable garden, blacksmith shop, icehouse, barn, and home—none of which remain today. Fortunately, Thoreau's prose preserved Smith's home for posterity. "It was a very spacious, low building," he wrote, "about eighty feet along, with many large apartments." Except for windows, materials were local. Logs were the chief ingredient: they were "posts, studes, boards, clapboards, laths, plaster, and nails, all in one." Thoreau found the architecture to be "a slight departure from the hollow tree." (124–127)

Smith earned his living by serving the lumber industry. He lodged and fed their men, as many as one hundred in winter. He cared for their beasts of burden. Tons of English hay were cut in his fields and stored in his barn for the horses and oxen. His smithy shod their feet, repaired their sleds, and provided other needed ironwork.

*Near the lake, which we were approaching with as much expectation as if it had been a university,—for it is not often that the stream of our life opens into such expansions,—were islands, and a low and meadowy shore with scattered trees, birches, white and yellow, slanted over the water, and maples,—many of the white birches killed, apparently by inundations. (122–123)*

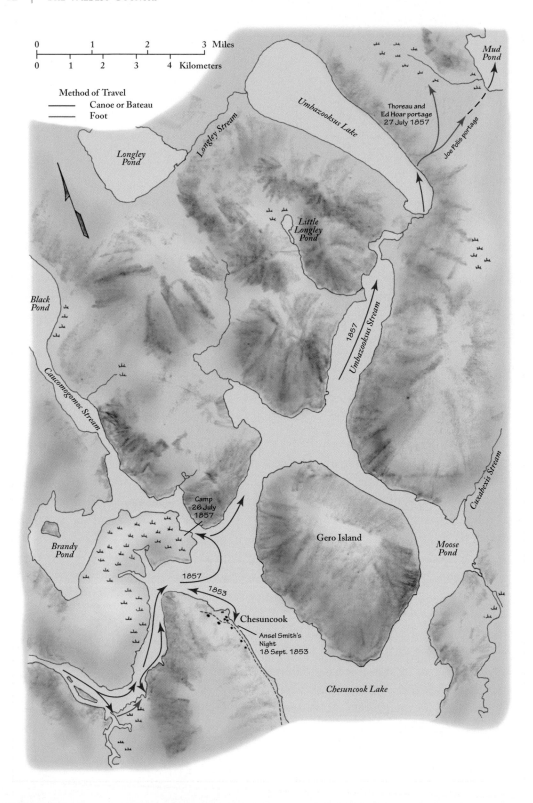

Ansel Smith (1815–1879) is buried in the village cemetery along with son Ansel B. Smith (1852–1927), both of whom managed the Chesuncook Lake House.

## Chesuncook Lake House, the McBurnies, and the Surprenants

"Such were the first rude beginnings of a town," Thoreau said of Ansel Smith's. (130) His prediction was correct. Where Ansel Smith lived is now the village of Chesuncook.

August 22, 1978, was a halcyon day, no clouds, no wind. Katahdin, thirty-five miles distant, was clearly visible from the Chesuncook Lake House (1864), to which we walked from the public landing. From 1957 until 1999, this hotel was owned and operated by the McBurnies. On that stunning day in 1978, Bert McBurnie was digging in his yard as we approached. "The back field of my dry well clogged," he explained while resting on his shovel. A trapper's son, Bert was born in Presque Isle, Maine, in

*The tombstone of Ansel Smith*

1931. He attended school in Chesuncook, learning his lessons in the small church which still stands there. "Three girls and me in class," he smiled, "a wonder I ever married." He did, but not one of his classmates. He met his wife, Maggie Darnis, in Paris, France, her birthplace. As he talked more about his travels in Europe and Alaska, we asked him if he ever desired to live anywhere else besides Chesuncook. His pipe slipped from one side of his mouth to the other. "No, never seen anybody I envy," he replied.

Bert McBurnie died at age sixty-six in April 1997. Maggie ran the inn until she sold it in 1999 to the Surprenants. At age seventy-two, she still prepares nourishing meals, now for vacationers at the Penobscot Lake Lodge, sixty miles northwest of Greenville, at the Quebec border.

David and Luisa Surprenant, of Mattapoisett, Massachusetts, on Buzzards Bay, with their five children, increased the hamlet's year-round population from four to eleven, Christine Schultz observed in a 2002 *Yankee* magazine article about Chesuncook Lake House. When

Tom Slayton, the former longtime Editor of *Vermont Life* Magazine visited in August 2006, he found them home-schooling their children, caring for guests, and serving scrumptious baked bread. On January 10, 2007, David reported to me that they had 5–6 inches of snow in a relatively snowless winter for New England, 7–8 inches of ice, and reservations for the upcoming weekend.

"How will they get there in winter?" I asked.

"Snowmobile."

"Over the lake?"

"No, by the road; it's about four miles."

Winter accommodations are in cabins for four. When the lake is iceless, usually from mid-May to mid-October, guests come up the lake by boat—David calls for them—or they fly in via Jack's of Greenville or Katahdin Air of Millinocket. Though open year-round, the Suprenants have time for themselves.

Spring fishing begins with the ice's departure, and the inn's four rooms fill. Electricity is by generator; evening parlor light by gas lamps; organic vegetables come from their garden. Reservations can be made by calling 207-745-5330 or online at chesuncooklakehouse.com.

## Caucomgomoc Stream

On his 1857 excursion, Thoreau returned to Chesuncook by the West Branch. This time he left northward through a wide estuary to Caucomgomoc Stream. After a short distance on the latter, he passed the mouth of Umbazooksus Stream.[4] He continued fol-

*The note of the white-throated sparrow, a very inspiriting but almost wiry sound, was the first heard in the morning, and with this all the woods sang. (193)*

*White-throated sparrow*

lowing the Caucomgomoc, however, for another half mile before stopping on its southern shore for the evening.

This was the Polis family hunting ground. The scene has changed since the last century. The party's camp now sits in a marsh. The falls immediately above them on the river has disappeared. Thoreau's wildflowers are gone. The present vegetation consists of grasses and dri-ki. (Dri-ki, or dry kill, is the dead vegetation standing along streams and lakes; it is killed by flooding.) Hoary stumps lie on their sides, dwarfed by their roots radiating into the air. Barkless, limbless trees stand like telephone poles awaiting their wires. Beyond the mire, the forest forms a green irregular horizon.

Just before dark, Thoreau saw a muskrat swimming down stream. Polis tried to kill the rodent by calling him closer. Thoreau thought their conversation amusing. Polis was "a wild man indeed, to be talking to a musquash! . . . He seemed suddenly to have quite forsaken humanity, and gone over to the musquash side." (206–207) The muskrat persisted in his course, apparently not in the mood for a powwow.

## Suggested Side Trip

A possible side trip explores Caucomgomoc Stream, which runs ten miles north through Black Pond to Caucomgomoc Lake. From the lake you can return the same way or go to Chamberlain Lake via Ciss Stream, Round Pond, and Allagash Lake and Stream. Reaching Allagash Lake from Round Pond requires a three-mile portage. Before tote service was provided across Mud Pond Carry, this way was used to reach Chamberlain Lake.[5]

I went this way in August 1980. A pair of great blue herons entertained me on Ciss Stream. Mud plantain bloomed on its banks. The portage from Round Pond into Allagash Lake, though mostly on lumber roads, exhausted

*Swamp milkweed*

Jerry and Marcy Monkman/EcoPhotography

*I plucked at the water's edge the Asclepias incarnata with quite handsome flowers, a brighter red than our variety (the pulchra). It was the only form of it which I saw there. (208)*

my group; we retraced our steps twice for packs and another canoe. Our efforts were rewarded, however, by raspberries and two moose, a cow and a calf, who also were munching these fruits. Allagash Mountain (1,809 feet), complete with fire tower, gave us a visual treat.

## Umbazooksus Stream

On July 27, 1857, Thoreau retraced the short segment of Caucomgomoc to its union with Umbazooksus, ascending the latter to the lake of the same name. "Much meadow river," Polis translated *Umbazooksus.* (207) The stream's setting confirmed its designation. Between its shore and the forest ran broad margins of sedges, wool-grass, and blue flag irises, with narrow-leaved willows and red osier dogwoods on higher ground.

You have to imagine this landscape today. The meadows have vanished; evergreens are close to the water's edge. Leaving Caucomgomoc, you now enter Chesuncook Lake, not Umbazooksus, and you stay in it for two and one-half miles while passing Gero Island to the east.

*Yellow clintonia*

### GERO ISLAND

Was Thoreau mistaken in believing that Chesuncook Lake was "without an island?" (123) No, his observation was correct. Gero's 3,185 acres were part of the mainland until 1916, when Ripogenus Dam forced their separation.

The property of the state of Maine, this island is managed by the Bureau of Public Lands as a multiple-use area; at one time, it was a game refuge, but no longer.[6] Four campsites are provided on the island's western shore.

Umbazooksus begins beyond Gero Island. For the next two and one-half miles it resembles lake, however, not stream. A narrow channel leads from the northern end of this bay. The entrance is marked by a wooden bridge under which canoes can usually be floated. Shortly, the way is blocked by a dilapidated crossing, which is best portaged. Beyond the environment is similar to what Thoreau experienced:

*The stream was only from one and one half to three rods wide, quite winding, with occasional small islands, meadows, and some very swift and shallow places. (210)*[7]

Finding high water, they used a black spruce pole to pole their way upstream; they had to get out to walk with their packs only once. Your voyage also depends on the water level. Ordinarily, canoes have to be hauled through the upper part of the stream. At the head of Umbazooksus, there is a sluice gate, a portage over the embankment, and two campsites—none of these mentioned by Thoreau.

---

## Maine Woods Teas

*I, for one, however, am not an old tea-drinker, and cannot speak with authority to others. (206)*

Admittedly, Thoreau was not a connoisseur of tea. He rarely indulged himself in that way: " . . . think of dashing the hopes of a morning with a cup of warm coffee, or of an evening with a dish of tea!"[8] "The poet," Thoreau believed, "postpones tea indefinitely." (August 11, 1853) To learn about his environment or simply to savor something other than lake water, however, caused him to set aside abstinence. When in Maine he did what was customary.

The essential beverage of the North Woods in his day was black tea. Loggers consumed vast quantities of it, plain or sweetened with molasses or sugar, at all meals. A pound of this staple

*Creeping snowberry*

*Teaberry*

accompanied Thoreau, Hoar, and Polis on their journey. Black tea was real tea, probably *Thea sinensis;* it contained caffeine and tannin, among other constituents. Coming from a shrub growing wild in northeastern India or cultivated in other Far East countries where climate permitted, it was imported to New England.

When Down East, Thoreau sampled this and other "teas." The latter were indigenous substitutes used frequently by the Indians. He was served at least four kinds—two heaths and two pines—and was introduced to more. All were common in Maine in the mid-nineteenth century, and still are today. Try them. See if your taste agrees with his.

## Heaths

### Creeping Snowberry, *Gualtheria hispidula*

*We could have had a new kind of tea every night.*
*(206)*

While camped at Caucomgomoc Stream on July 27, Polis brought Thoreau a fragile vine with tiny evergreen leaves and white fruits. He called it *cowosnebagosar,* translated "grows where trees have rotted," and asked Thoreau what it was. The botanist replied with an equally odd

*Labrador tea*

locution: *Chiogenes* (now *Gaultheria*) *hispidula,* and added its very common name, creeping snow-berry. He had seen it everywhere, especially thriving under spruces and firs. Polis said that it "made the best tea of anything in the woods"—much better than black tea. (206) After tasting some and enjoying its wintergreen flavor, Thoreau agreed that it was his favorite tea, too.

### Teaberry or Checkerberry, *Gaultheria procumbens*
Four nights later, Polis made his companions another refreshment. This one was teaberry or *Gualtheria procumbens,* an herb which looks similar to its relative. It also bears tasty red fruits in autumn. Thoreau liked its wintergreen essence and named their camp on the East Branch in its honor. Euell Gibbons suggests letting this drink stand in a closed jar for a few days. The fermentation enhances its flavor, while adding more leaves does not. Gibbons also offers recipes for wine, syrup, and candy—hardly trail creations, but you might want to test them at home.

Both *Gaultherias* are also popularly called wintergreen because of their aroma. Thoreau, however, reserved this common name for pipsissewa, *Chimaphila umbellata,* a member of the wintergreen family, along with the pyrolas, which he also found in Maine.

### *Labrador Tea, Ledum groenlandicum*
Another drink that Polis proposed was Labrador tea. This heath, common to Maine's bogs and mountains, is easily distinguished by its woolly leaves that roll their edges under to touch their rusty bottoms. Though there is no record of Thoreau having sampled any, I cannot imagine his

*Eastern hemlock*

Photo by Ben Kimball for the NH Natural Heritage Bureau

*Northern white cedar*

resisting the invitation. After his last trip on the Penobscot, he discovered this plant for the first time in Concord on February 4, 1858. He named its habitat "Ledum Swamp."

## Pine Family Members

**Eastern Hemlock,** *Tsuga canadensis*
The morning after leaving Checkerberry-tea Camp, Thoreau had hemlock-needle tea instead of coffee for breakfast. This was not the poison hemlock, *Conium maculatum,* which killed Socrates, but *Tsuga canadensis,* the only hemlock native to Maine—though some Carolina hemlock has been planted. "Tolerable," Thoreau judged. Since Thoreau gave no hint of its flavor, I wanted to sample it. Aside from a prominent piney fragrance, it is bland and rather pleasant, though not as good as the heaths.

A shade, rock, and water lover, this evergreen adorns Maine's ravines and rivers where in winter, Thoreau observed, "it concentrates in itself the beauty of all fluviatile trees." (April 1, 1852) Polis told Thoreau that Allagash meant "hemlock bark." (323) Better known for its bark than its beverage, hemlock provided tannin for treating leather, an industry which flourished in Maine from shortly after Thoreau's last visit to the 1890s.

## Northern White-Cedar, Eastern Arbor-Vitae, *Thuja occidentalis*

*"A quart of arbor-vitae, To make him strong and mighty," (55)*

So went the verse of lumberers, who steeped the foliage of this prevalent evergreen. It would be interesting to know whether they consumed this amount, and what the effect was. I rather suspect that a draught of this size would leave one weak and nauseous, not strong and mighty, but I am not about to experiment. Like Thoreau, I found one taste enough. Actually, many rheumatics swear that cedar tea has helped them. After drinking some, Euell Gibbons remarked that he almost preferred the disease.

What this conifer lacks in flavor, it makes up for in utility. Local residents showed Thoreau its many purposes, to wit: cambium for emergency food; wood for canoe gunwales and planking, as well as carrying yokes; bark for tumplines, cords, and straps—arbor-vitae held moose hides to drying racks—and boughs for twig brooms, or besoms, and beds—Thoreau selected these twigs to sleep on instead of spruce, relishing their "strawberry" air. The tree's versatility so impressed Thoreau that he later realized:

*How little I know of that* arbor-vitae *when I have learned only what science can tell me! It is but a word. It is not a tree of life. But there are twenty words for the tree and its different parts which the Indians gave, which are not in our botanies, which imply more practical and vital science. (March 5, 1858)*

## Other Possible "Teas"

Two other conifers of this area that you might like are black spruce, *Picea mariana,* and white pine, *Pinus strobus.* (For more on these trees, see Chapter Seven.) Thoreau tried the former's needles in Concord on February 4, 1858, the same day he discovered *Ledum.* "In spite of a slight piny or turpentine flavor," he thought it "unexpectedly good." The young tips of spruce boughs were used for making beer. Many a Mainer was raised on spruce beer, as was Robert P. Tristam Coffin, who remembered that "it tasted wild."[9] White pine needles are rich in vitamins A and C. If you cannot take pleasure in their flavor, you can in knowing that you body is being nourished. There will be no scurvy on this trip! With a dash of lemon and sugar, Gibbons rated the brew "almost enjoyable." I have had a cup each day while writing this book, and have acquired a taste for it.

### American Pennyroyal, *Hedeoma pulegioides*
Members of the mint family also make delicious teas and tisanes, or medicinal beverages. Dried leaves of American pennyroyal, a common herb of dry fields and meadows, are especially flavorful. Thoreau, however, after drinking some in Concord, did not think so; like arbor-vitae, for him its taste was "too medicinal." (September 22, 1856) Do not feel at a loss should you not desire pennyroyal as a tea. This annual has other attributes. Put a snipping in your shirt pocket or in your sleeping bag for a perfume or a deodorant. Rub it on your skin to keep mosquitoes away. Apparently, Thoreau, who was well acquainted with this plant, never knew of this latter purpose. While in the North Woods, his insect repellent consisted of a wash of "sweet-oil and oil of turpentine, with a little oil of spearmint, and camphor," a frightening mixture, which, after applying, he concluded "was worse than the disease." (214)

The Maine woods, as you can see, are full of varieties of tea substitutes. Those suggested here are but a few of nature's gifts. Always make sure, however, that what you drink is safe. Wild strawberry and raspberry leaves are pleasing but, Euell Gibbons warns, must be dried completely to expel any toxins before being decocted.

*[T]he country is virtually unmapped and unexplored,*
*and there still waves the virgin forest of the New World. (83)*

## CHAPTER 5
# Allagash Lakes

## Mud Pond Carry, 1.75 Miles

A short paddle (³/₄ mile) across the southeast end of Umbazooksus Lake brings you to the portage to Mud Pond. Of the sixty-nine mud ponds in Maine, this one is the most famous, or infamous, because of the reputation of the land between it and Umbazooksus—"the wettest carry in the State," as Polis characterized it. (211) So it remains. The path is literally a narrow streambed, eroded well below the earth's surface. You try to stay on the banks, but eventually slip into the center and then slurp back onto higher ground. This happens several times. Finally conceding, you slosh through the channel, fearful that its bottom will inhale you. A little over halfway across, you notice that the flow over your sneakers has changed direction. It now runs northeast to Mud Pond and Chamberlain Lake. You have entered the Allagash watershed.[1] A soggy divide, indeed.

Your journey, nevertheless, is a holiday compared to Thoreau's. He and Ed Hoar got lost. They started on the correct trail, turned onto a supply road, crossed two streams, and waded knee-deep through two swamps—all with heavy packs, Hoar continually moving one ahead and going back for the other. Finally, after five miles, countless black flies, and Polis's guidance, they walked into Chamberlain Lake up to their waists to wash just before dark. They never saw Mud Pond. "Strange," Polis muttered, not understanding why they could not follow his tracks.[2] Thoreau remained cheerful: "I would not have missed that walk for a good deal." (221)

There was at least one compensation. Thoreau's introduction to low or swamp birch, *Betula pumila,* inspired him to christen the bog for the tree.[3] So as not to be reminded of the muck, I renamed this portage after jewelweed, *Impatiens capensis,* which thrives in this wetland and whose juice has cured my poison ivy.

It is impossible to lose your way on Jewelweed Carry today. The trail is too distinctive. There is only one turnoff: a lumber road completed by Great Northern in 1974–1975 intersects the path a quarter mile from Umbazooksus Lake. When you reach Mud Pond, you will find a campsite.

*. . . We entered on a level and very wet and rocky path through the universal dense evergreen forest, a loosely paved gutter. . . (212)*

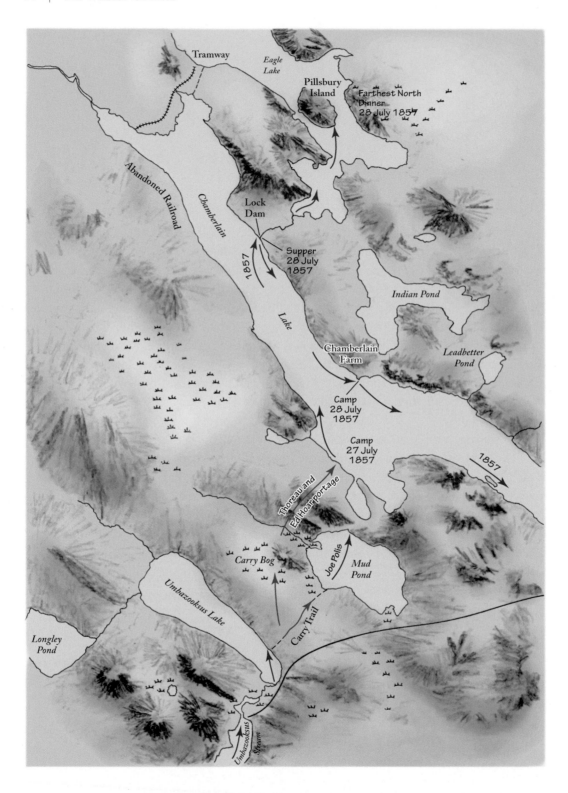

## Mud Pond, 1.25 Miles

Mud Pond is dying. Decaying matter—into which you launch your canoe—is competing for dominion over its waters. Twelve feet is its maximum depth, but four feet or less is the average over your course straight across to the outlet. Mats of aquatic vegetation, appearing as permanent islands, wait just below or on the surface. Lily pads darken the bottom, while their yellow and white flowers brighten the air. Canoeists need ingenuity to gain their destination in this milieu.

*It was a cedar swamp, through which the peculiar note of the white-throated sparrow rang loud and clear. There grew . . . what was new to me, the Low Birch (Betula pumila) a little rounded-leafed shrub, two or three feet high only. We thought to name this swamp after (it). (216–217)*

## Mud Pond Brook, .3 Mile

A small stone and log dam, about one and a half feet high, helps sustain Mud Pond. With encouragement canoes can be pulled over its spillway. You are now in Mud Pond Brook,

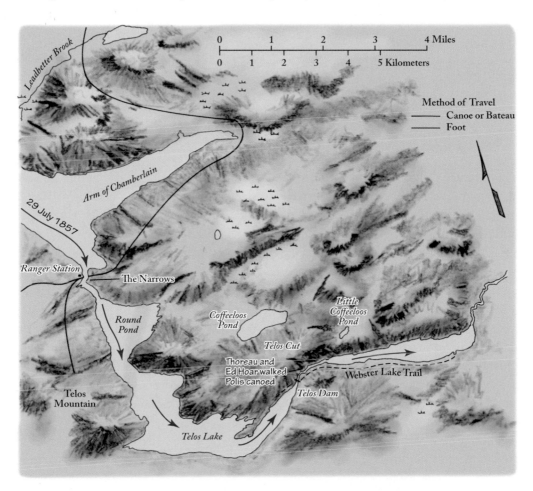

a short and shallow defile, which is best negotiated by walking, canoes in tow, though people have told me of their running its entire length in autumn.

## Chamberlain Lake

*We did not now intend to go far down the Allagash, but merely to get a view of the great lakes which are its source. . . . (227)*

Thoreau spent two nights on Chamberlain Lake. From his first camp on its west shore above Mud Pond Brook, he could look across the water to his next one, Chamberlain Farm. Instead of paddling directly there, he separated his sleeps with a fourteen-mile cruise to Eagle Lake and back.

The idea of staying on Chamberlain Lake with a day trip to Eagle Lake is appealing, though there is no reason not to stop on Eagle Lake itself. I have enjoyed a circular tour, which proceeds from Chamberlain over Lock Dam to Eagle Lake and returns to Chamberlain via the tramway (with its half-mile portage)—or, you can go in reverse.

## Lock Dam

*It is remarkable how little these important gates to a lake are blazoned. There is no triumphal arch over the modest inlet or outlet, but at some undistinguished point it trickles in or out through the uninterrupted forest, almost as through a sponge. (227–228)*

For centuries Chamberlain Lake flowed northward to Eagle Lake and then the Allagash and St. John rivers. In the spring of 1841, this direction was changed when Major Hastings Strickland of Bangor erected a dam at Chamberlain Lake's natural outlet. Later, a second dam was installed below the first, creating a lock for the purpose of elevating timber from Eagle into Chamberlain. Thoreau carried around the first dam, a predecessor of the current model, and, in a quarter of a mile, the lower one, which no longer exists; then he "walked about half a mile to lighten the canoe."[4] (230)

On the south side of Lock Dam there is a campsite where Thoreau had supper on July 28, 1857. Leave the lake here, and either enter the stream at the base of the dam, from thence running some easy rapids, or portage half a mile to still water.

Just north of the dam, a modest one-room, green-faced cabin hides at the edge of the woods. This was once the residence of Dorothy and Milford Kidney, who lived here from the late spring until late fall of each year from 1959. Their other home was in Yarmouth, Maine.

Milford had two employers. He watched the forest for the Allagash Wilderness Waterway and the dam for the East Branch Improvement Company. Unless he was fighting a brush fire or reporting the weather to Bangor over his two-way radio, he greeted you with a smile, told you about the moose he had seen and the fish he caught, collected your park fee, and gave you a map, trash bag, and some of Chamberlain's water to ease your passage down the stream to Eagle.

Indoors, Dorothy wrote. Already, she had hung the wash to dry, baked a fresh blueberry pie on her woodstove, and served us coffee. Articles, short stories, and novels poured from her pen. A bureau beside her bed displayed some of her work—it was the only bookstore in Allagash. She gave us a copy of her *Speaking of Miracles* to ingest while camping.

Together the Kidneys expressed a deep love for the wilderness, humanity, simplicity, God, and each other.

## Eagle Lake (Formerly Heron Lake)

From Lock Dam, Thoreau proceeded to the southeast end of Pillsbury Island, where he ate dinner on July 28, 1857. This campsite is now named for Thoreau. After botanizing and waiting out a thundershower, he and his party retraced their course to Chamberlain Lake.

## Eagle Lake Tramway and Railroad

This region offers a graphic example of twentieth-century lumbering practices. Between Eagle and Chamberlain lakes, a short and low divide separates the St. John and Penobscot watersheds. The desire to take timber from the former to the latter led to the mechanization of the land.

A giant conveyor chain spanned the divide first. In six years of operation, from 1902 to 1907, the tramway unpretentiously hauled one hundred million board feet from lake to lake. The solid apparatus—two eight-ton wood-burning boilers and a fourteen-ton steel cable upon which saddles for logs were clamped—was freighted by train from Bangor to Greenville and from there by ferry over Thoreau's route to the upper end of Chamberlain,

*Logging from bateau, circa 1900*

Patten Lumberman's Museum, Patten, Maine

where it was put in place over the crossing—a Herculean task. If it is difficult to imagine this load being transported in, it is easy to understand why it was never shipped out. This obsolete system still assumes its anomalous position, though its domain is disputed by an encroaching forest which now grows between the tracks. At Chamberlain Lake the boilers rest, and rust.

The weight of this equipment, however, is slight compared to that of its successors. Walking along the path a short distance from Eagle Lake, I was surprised by two ninety-ton locomotives. There is no signal, no station, no engineers, not even any track—just twin black steam engines that are going nowhere. For a decade, from 1927 to 1937, they labored, chugging through the woods back and forth between Chamberlain and Umbazooksus lakes—12.5 miles one way—on each trip drawing twelve cars filled with pulp-wood. You can still see where they went. A quarter mile north of the tramway is the start of their roadbed, now ensconced in raspberries and goldenrods. Their ruined trestle spans the mouth of Allagash Stream. Along Chamberlain's west side, the ties rot amid lanes which spruce cover. Their trestle which extended six hundred feet into Umbazooksus Lake to ease their unloading, is gone.[5]

## CHAMBERLAIN FARM AND THE NUGENTS

> *The Chamberlain Farm is no doubt a cheerful opening in the woods, but such was the late-ness of the hour that it has left but a dusky impression on my mind. (240)*

The Thoreau party ate its supper at Lock Dam, while the rain abated. Between storms, the men paddled 3.5 miles through choppy water to Chamberlain Farm, arriving in darkness. From shoreline to hilltop ran a spacious clearing—some six hundred acres in the 1880s—which was the first on the lake, dating to 1846. Like Ansel Smith's, its mission was to sup-ply the logging operation, which had intensified in the area during that decade. Cattle and sheep grazed; oats, hay, potatoes, and vegetables ripened in the sun; and, an apple orchard produced succulent fruit.[6]

A storehouse there provided goods to transients throughout the nineteenth century. Thoreau asked for sugar. They had consumed their six pounds in five days! "It was no wonder," Thoreau laughed, "for Polis had a sweet tooth. He would first fill his dipper nearly a third full of sugar, and then add coffee to it." (239) He was sold four pounds of brown sugar at twenty cents a pound—all that could be spared.

The sweetness found here today is in the scene. The sweep of space is over the lake, not the land. Woods and wildflowers have reclaimed the fields. Cabins have replaced ag-riculture. Patty Nugent managed this camp and the one three miles east, a task she per-formed jointly with her husband, Al ("Nuge") until his death on February 10, 1978. Patty passed away in 1990.

The Nugents were twentieth-century pioneers of the Allagash. They came into the country in July 1936, when they were in their early thirties, wanting a better deal than the

Depression offered. Wilderness required no mortgages, only persistence, enterprise, and courage—qualities the Nugents had in abundance. They arrived on the shores of Telos Lake from East Millinocket over the Nesowadnehunk Trail. They hand-hewed logs for a raft, packed all their possessions aboard, and floated off in search of a home. Settling on Chamberlain Lake, they built a shelter of driftwood and planted a garden. Their first winter would have claimed less dedicated souls. They breathed January air at -50°F. Dressed for the outdoors, they ate indoors, huddled by the woodstove. They talked to each other or to themselves, for no one else was near. Nuge also talked to the animals. He fished and hunted, not even the deepest snow preventing his checking his traps, which extended far into the forest. At last, the sun grew stronger, ice melted, and birches budded. The Nugents stayed and went on raising vegetables, building cabins, and tracking fur.

On Saturday morning, August 13, 1983, we spontaneously stopped at Chamberlain Farm to see Patty Nugent, who would be seventy-nine at the end of October. Graciously, she put tea and coffee on the dining room table. "You caught me without fresh milk; it just went sour. I do have cream." For forty-seven years, this had been her home. "I could give you a piece of raspberry pie. Kind of early in the morning." It's never too early for fresh raspberry pie. She put the pie and two platefuls of ten donuts on the table. "I think you are hungry." She asked her helper, Tom, to be sure to pick more berries that day.

Ice had cleared the lake in May, we heard, and the previous spring "a twister smashed porches and windows of three cabins on the eastern end," Patty said. "How about more donuts? They would be better if we warmed 'em up for you."

Such was the legendary hospitality of Chamberlain Farm of Patty Nugent and her husband, Al. You will enjoy reading about them and Chamberlain Farm in Dean Bennett's fine book (see Further Reading). The camps are still open to the public. You can contact managers John Richardson and Regina Webster at 207-944-5991 or visit www.nugent-mcnallycamps.com.

On July 29, 1857, Thoreau left Chamberlain Farm under cloudy but dry skies. He was anxious to cross the placid lake before it roiled. The party breakfasted on a rocky point, the first that appears on the opposite shore below the two bays. This is not a campsite, not even much of a stopping place.

## The Narrows

Completing their crossing of Chamberlain, they passed through the Narrows, now a hub of activity. There are two campsites, one on either side, a Maine warden's office on the south shore, and beyond that the Allagash Wilderness Waterway headquarters, from which canoe trips regularly depart. In 1966, the Maine State Legislature, compensating paper companies $3 million for their lands (the federal government provided half), ensured that the Allagash River from Telos Lake to the St. John River would remain in its natural state—the first act of river conservation in America. The concern now is to protect this hundred-mile preserve from the multitudes who seek to enjoy it.

Part of this responsibility falls on the users, part on the park rangers. Skip and Shirley Cram were once stationed here six months of the year to maintain the integrity of the Allagash. The chain saws we heard in the distance, they assured us, were Canadians cutting private timber; the public domain remains untouched. In the late nineteenth century, men from the Maritime Provinces found employment in the Maine woods. Receiving less pay than Yankee laborers, they depressed wages and incurred the hostility of their competitors. Why do they still lumber here? "They are the best," Skip Cram testifies. "We've had 'em all up here—from India, Norway, Sweden. No one cuts wood like the Canadians. On clearing land for Highway 95, they cut two acres a day to our half acre. They earned $275 an acre, though most of that went for their skidders."

Chamberlain Bridge spans the strait in front of the park entrance. At one time, a Great Northern camp sat just north of it at Coffeelos. Late in the morning of August 13, 1976, Charles Graham, who had been a Great Northern employee since 1941, left Coffeelos and drove across the bridge on his way to Greenville. Interested in comparing nineteenth- and twentieth-century lumberers, I asked him about his life.

> Graham: *A cook, assistant cook, and KP person prepare two meals a day. There is always a pot of beans for breakfast; eggs, potatoes, and bacon. We pack our own lunches. For dinner, pies, chicken, and steak once a week.*

> Thoreau: *The logger's fare consists of tea, molasses, flour, pork,—sometimes beef,—and beans. (20)*

> Graham: *We live in a trailer, banked in sawdust and heated with oil, it is warm.*

> Thoreau: *These camps were about twenty feet long by fifteen feet wide, built of logs . . . with the bark on; . . . The chimney was an oblong square hole in the middle . . . The interstices were filled with moss, and the roof was shingled with long and handsome splints of cedar, or spruce, or pine. . . .These houses are made comfortable by the huge fires that can be afforded night and day. (19)*

> Graham: *I come in on Sunday night from Greenville. Work four ten-hour days and five hours on Friday, quitting at 11:00 a.m. I operate a bulldozer, clearing roads. At night we talk, watch TV, or play billiards.*

> Thoreau: *The driver works as long as he can see, from dark to dark, and at night has not time to eat his supper and dry his clothes fairly, before he is asleep on his cedar bed. (76)*

## Telos Lake and Dam

Thoreau noticed his first red pines in Maine on Telos Lake's northeast shore. He could have inspected them on either of two adjacent points, where they still grow. My guess is that he stopped at the eastern point.

Arriving at the dam, which was built in March 1841, he met Allan B. Farrar, the damkeeper and "solitary hunter" who occupied a log hut nearby.[7] (243)

Telos Dam has a tradition of solitary supervisors. When the new dam was completed in October 1941, a century after the first structure was built, Clair R. Desmond came from the Maine Forest Service to

*Common loon*

oversee it. A strong, independent, and frugal man with a wealth of woods lore, weather savvy, and travel tips, Clair admirably filled the role. For the next thirty-five years, the Allagash was his world. He never left, except for an occasional visit to Bangor. When we passed through on August 11, 1976, I missed his friendly welcome. Four days earlier he had died at the age of seventy-nine.

In the fall of 1976, Jim Drake succeeded Clair Desmond. At fifty-seven, Jim was no novice backwoodsman. As an Allagash ranger for six years and as assistant to James Erwin at his Long Pond sporting camp for a decade, Jim was well-prepared for the job. Like those before him, he lived alone at Telos Dam, throughout the seasons, caring for the country.

## Telos Cut

*The rush of the water has produced such changes in the canal that it has now the appearance of a very rapid mountain stream flowing through a ravine, and you would not suspect that any digging had been required to persuade the waters of the St. John to flow into the Penobscot here. (245)*

The Allagash and Penobscot valleys embrace in a narrow passage between Telos and Webster lakes. Thoreau, Hubbard, and others have referred to this nexus as a canal. Fannie Hardy Eckstorm disagreed: "It is not a 'canal' in any sense, but a 'cut,' a wild mountain torrent."[8] It is both, in fact—an artificial and natural waterway.

Nature required minimum adjustment for man's design here. When Chamberlain's water was high enough, it normally spilled into the ravine and trickled down to Webster Lake. An increased flow and some prodding would enable logs to go this way to Bangor instead of by the Allagash-St. John rivers to Canadian mills. In the spring of 1841, the completion of Telos and Lock dams provided the thrust that made the shorter trip possible. Other modifications improved the course. That autumn a trench—10–15 feet wide by 480 feet long—was dug in front of Telos Dam, and that winter, 1841–1842, earth was removed from behind the dam and a swath of trees felled along the line to Webster Lake. By spring, the channel was set to accommodate its passengers—nine million feet of timber bumped through that year.

No sooner was this dream realized than a human obstacle arose. The new owner of the Telos property, Rufus Dwinel of Bangor, levied a toll on lumber using his sluiceway. Drivers protested his high rates, probably threatening force to deliver their goods. Dwinel hired security guards to defend his rights. The lumbermen appealed to Maine state legislators, who in August 1846 settled the dispute. This incident is called the "Telos War," undoubtedly an exaggeration of the strifeless, bloodless disagreement between two parties.

On July 29, 1857, Thoreau and Hoar walked three-quarters of a mile from Telos to Webster Lake, while Polis canoed down the "rapid and rocky river." (247)

Similar options exist today. Once beyond the dam, either ground or water transportation is available to Webster Lake. From a dock on the east (right) shore of Telos Lake, you follow the driveway to the damtender's residence. When the road turns to the house, go straight across the lawn into the woods, where a jeep trail leads to Webster Lake. Shortly, on the west (left), trees with red paint designate the path to the stream. Choose your mentor: Polis or Thoreau.

---

## Maine Woods Birds

**Common Loon,** *Gavia immer*
Of all the birds of Maine that Thoreau became acquainted with, none seemed more symbolic of wilderness than common loons, which appeared to him on every lake. They were Thoreau's

constant traveling companions. Though their numbers have decreased since the 1850s due to pollution, human and animal nest predation, and loss of nest habitat, they are not rare. With few exceptions, I saw them in the 1970s on all the lakes Thoreau visited.

Like moose, loons love solitude. They seldom congregate, except to migrate. Ordinarily, they swim in pairs. One family prefers a lake to itself, or at least a sizable portion of a large body of water. Dressed in summer in a black cap with white neck scarf and piebald cape, they move almost invisibly across dark waters. Sometimes these solitary hunters swim with only their bills exposed, like submarine periscopes scanning their surroundings.

Three traits distinguish loons—their meteorological sense, their peculiar sounds, and their Olympic swimming. These attributes have earned them the respective nicknames of rain goose, lonely yodeler, and great northern diver.

## Rain Goose

For a long time, loons have been recognized as weather-breeders. Scots, on the remote and rocky Shetland Isles, christened the red-throated loon "rain goose," invariably connecting its call with foul skies. The Penobscots believed the same thing. Polis told Thoreau that the common loon, *medawisla* in his language, signified wind. (165) Already Thoreau had experienced their portending power at Walden Pond. On a calm October day of perfect "autumnal tints,"

*A pair of loons*

a loon's cry summoned an east wind laden with precipitation. (October 8, 1852) While cross-ing Moosehead Lake, James Russell Lowell learned about their weather-predicting ability from a Mainer and witnessed an appropriate demonstration of it.[9] Later in the century, more cre-dence was lent to this tradition by the studies of Cambridge ornithologist William Brewster. At Umbagog Lake on the Maine-New Hampshire border, his guides informed him that the loon's wail during an absolutely still day "after a prolonged silence on the part of the bird" meant an approaching wind. Though skeptical at first, after almost forty years at Umbagog, Brewster seldom found the prophecy of the birds to be wrong.[10]

## Lonely Yodeler

You cannot camp on the shore of the Maine lakes that Thoreau traveled without at least hearing the loon's call. "A very wild sound," Thoreau characterized it, "quite in keeping with the place and the circumstances of the traveller and very unlike the voice of a bird. I could lie awake for hours listening to it, it is so thrilling." (223–224)

This voice is the bird's hallmark. It hoots through the early morning mist. You cannot see the signaler for the steam, can only hear *hoo-hoo-hoo*, once, twice, three times, penetrating the vapor, like an actor rehearsing offstage before the curtain rises. After adroitly eluding you in the water, the loon surfaces beside you and laughs. He also wails at sunset. A medley from afar, shrill and startling, its source unknown, ends your evening reverie. Any of these howls may incite a response from some distance, then another reply and another, until a continual falsetto chorus reverberates through the wilds—a concert in your chambers. Then, as suddenly as the music started, it stops. You are left alone to ponder the meaning of these messages.

## Great Northern Diver

As divers loons are peerless. No ducks can surpass them—neither grebe nor merganser. They swim far, fast, and deep. They descend instantly and quietly, driven by their big feet and legs. Depths of 200 feet are not unknown to them.

On land their mobility is another matter entirely. This is a foreign planet to them. Walking is impossible. They stumble along, flopping on their stomachs. A liquid runway is needed to become airborne. Even then, rising is helped by a breeze, and the stronger the better.

They submerge for escape, food, and fun. Their great underwater speed enables them to easily catch their meals. They dine on fish, whatever varieties are available, and crayfish. Loons revel in the water. Thoreau observed an amusing display of their talent at Walden:

*So long-winded was he and so unweariable, that when he had swum farthest he could immediately plunge again, nevertheless; and then no wit could divine where in the deep pond, beneath the smooth surface, he might be speeding his way . . .*[11]

As you paddle along, watch out for the antics of the loon. You may even see one wave a foot at you! Thoreau did. (33)

*[W]e shot up the rapids like a salmon, the water rushing and roaring around,
so that only a practiced eye could distinguish a safe course . . . (32)*

CHAPTER 6
# Webster Lake and Brook

## Webster Lake

Below Telos Cut lies Webster Lake, a dark blue thoroughfare extending eastward almost three miles to feed Webster Brook. This strand of water, with its forested shore, untenanted except for a few rustic cabins, conveys a sense of primitiveness today. Webster Lake and Brook are still the most remote parts of Thoreau's journey. Compared to the Allagash, few canoers go this way.

Joe Polis called Webster Lake *Madunkehunk-gamooc*, "height of land pond"; he omitted the suffix when speaking of the stream. This name was geographically correct until 1841, when Chamberlain Lake was moved into the Penobscot watershed. Another Penobscot Indian, John Pennowit, told Hubbard that Webster Lake was known as *Kwanosagamaik*, meaning "'peaked pond,' i.e., pointed at each end."[1] This description fits Webster Lake, whose widest part—barely one-half mile—occurs near the center, and whose extremities contract. In form and function this lake resembles a pipette, a slender tube transferring solutions from one river basin to the other.

When Thoreau reached the eastern end of Webster Lake, there was a dam, at which he ate dinner, and an abandoned loggers' camp, neither of which are in evidence today. Nearby, to the south, is the Webster Lake Outlet Campsite, with good swimming from a sand beach. Behind the campsite a short path connects with the Freezeout Trail heading east, or with the Webster Lake Trail.

## Webster Brook

*It is exceedingly rapid and rocky, and also shallow, and can hardly be considered navigable, unless that may mean that what is launched in it is sure to be carried swiftly down it, though it may be dashed to pieces by the way. It is somewhat like navigating a thunder-spout. (249)*

Joe Polis shot the "thunder-spout" in his bark canoe, while Thoreau and Hoar, baggage in hand, followed oxen and moose tracks over a "wild woodpath." (250) Their way approximates that of the contemporary Freezeout Trail, which runs 7.8 miles between Webster Lake and Grand Lake Matagamon. When we went over this trail in August 1978, it was

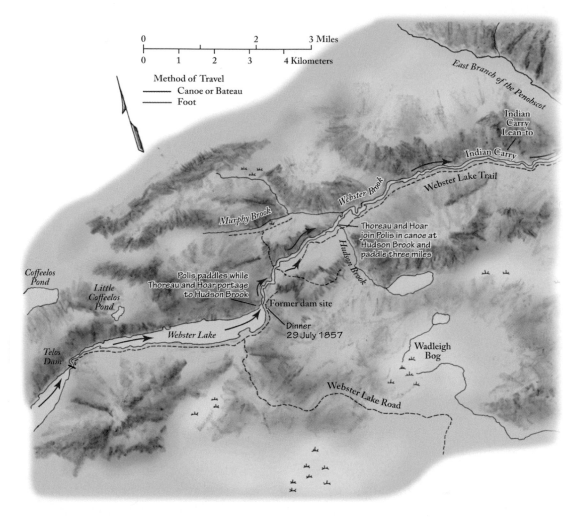

0       2     3 Miles

0   1   2   3    4 Kilometers

Method of Travel
——— Canoe or Bateau
——— Foot

East Branch of the Penobscot

Indian Carry Lean-to

Indian Carry

Webster Lake Trail

*Webster Brook*

*Murphy Brook*

Thoreau and Hoar join Polis in canoe at Hudson Brook and paddle three miles

*Hudson Brook*

Coffeelos Pond

Little Coffeelos Pond

Polis paddles while Thoreau and Hoar portage to Hudson Brook

Former dam site

Dinner 29 July 1857

Webster Lake

Wadleigh Bog

Telos Dam

Webster Lake Road

barely discernable in places; especially rough going was the mouth of Hudson Brook, through which we had to bushwhack. A year later, a complete transformation had occurred. Thanks to Baxter State Park workers, the path was cleared and blazed with blue paint; sections were relocated to follow the river's high banks; and signs and lean-tos were installed.

Webster Brook displays a variety of moods. No two points on its façade appear alike. Similarly, the same place in different seasons, on different days, even at different hours, may not be recognizable. This mutable character results from the amount of water entering, which is determined by precipitation, by Telos Dam, and by the nature of the stream—its gradient, the material of its bed and bank, the shape of its channel, and the kinds of sediment transported. Getting to know Webster Brook requires patience.

On August 12, 1976, Webster Brook was more excited than I ever recalled seeing it. For the last three days, tropical storm Belle had saturated the Maine woods with wind and

rain. The Allagash below Long Lake was flooded and closed to canoers; bridges were awash. Unknown to us—since we had camped during the storm on Webster Lake—three gates of Telos Dam were opened that morning to discharge the excess water from Chamberlain Lake. We entered the current without fully realizing its force. There were no small standing waves, only huge piles of foam which slapped our bow and leaped into our boat. We tried to hold a course over the crests of the combers, but were pushed askew. Three heads ducked as we went too close to shore, branches sweeping over us, jostling at our sides; one removed my sunglasses and tossed them into the rampaging stream. We steered for a place to land, passing beyond before we were near it. We tried again, with the same result. Finally, cast into bushes, we gained a hold on terra firma. Dripping-wet packs were heaved ashore; the canoe was hauled out and turned over— its contents running back into the river. Then we returned to the tempest.

You can expect to see similar turbulence. The first 6.5 miles from Webster Lake to Indian Carry are mostly shallow rapids and fast current. This stretch is in medium water and is an excited rapid that can be run by experts. However, it requires very difficult maneuvering, and it is recommended that this drop be carried on the right bank.

Polis enjoyed different conditions. When the water calmed, Polis stopped and took aboard his passengers, the older of whom related his feeling about canoeing: "It is very exhilarating . . . coasting down this inclined mirror, which was now and then gently winding, down a mountain, indeed, between two evergreen forests, edged with lofty dead white pines. . . ." (252) Tall white pines, most of them alive, are still present, though they are not the predominant border tree.

After the Indian Carry Lean-to is passed on the south (right) shore, the stream in the next two miles before Grand Pitch drops over low ledges. Scout all of these before proceeding. Assess their impact in relation to your skill and fortitude, and to your canoe's load and fabric. All of these rapids can be run with extreme caution. Portages go around each. Their starts, marked by red crosses or squares painted on rocks or ribbons tied to branches, are all on the south (right) shore. Usually, three carries are made, each about a quarter of a mile. These blazed paths, which are not part of Freezeout Trail, are becoming increasingly confined by underbrush.

"Coming to falls and rapids, our easy progress was suddenly terminated," Thoreau groaned. Polis instructed his crew: "'You got to walk; ver strong water.'" (253) Ashore they met encumbrances: " . . . fallen and drifted trees and bushes, and rocks, from time to time swinging ourselves round over the water, or else taking to a gravel bar or going inland." (254) While Hoar found a bridge on which to cross a deep tributary, Thoreau navigated it nude.

Fannie Hardy Eckstorm, who walked from lake to lake in September 1888, remarked on the personality of this byway:

> The road grew worse,—Mud Pond Carry in double installments, mud and water everywhere but with stretches of good road on higher land. There were continual signs of lumbering. . . . [2]

A forest fire, in 1855 Thoreau believed, had ravaged the landscape here. Exposed was the bare relief, a series of rocky ledges and ravines over which they struggled. From higher elevations, Grand Lake Matagamon was visible three miles distant. Among the charred trunks, blueberries, raspberries, and pink and white fireweeds redecorated the earth. "This burnt land" affected Thoreau as being "exceedingly wild and desolate." (255)

As I walked along here, my predecessor's sense of desolation was gone. The holocaust had healed. The woods, regenerated, were healthy, vigorous. The boreal flora thrived. Tall spruce rose from the sides of the path, spires touching the sky. From lower branches, usnea lichens hung like drying cloths; green-gray light filtered through their webs. Familiar bunchberry, *Cornus canadensis*, was in red fruit. Growing just below my knees was another common woodland herb, wild sarsaparilla, *Aralia nudicaulis*, whose chopped roots Indians steeped for tea. Sarsaparilla's generous brown leaves attracted the eye in a wilderness of green life. This August it was the first plant hereabouts to wear its autumnal attire.

While immersed in this burnt region, the two foot travelers separated. Hoar plunged ahead, while Thoreau went to help Polis, who was straining to get his canoe through the torrent. Returning, Thoreau could not locate Hoar anywhere: "It was as if he had sunk into the earth." (258) Darkness ended an unsuccessful search and forced them to camp apart. Polis and Thoreau crossed to the "eastern or smoother side" of the stream, where they slept close to the falls which "shook the earth under us."[3] (260)

The climax of Webster Brook occurs in three movements. Each expresses its own sound and spirit. The introduction is allegro. A narrow channel receives peaceful waters and churns them into white lather before letting go. The middle is crescendo. Twin jets spray over a sixteen-foot-high ledge, project light and thunder, and faint into a quiet pool. The finale is scherzo. The happy current alternates between agitated and relaxed moods until it subsides. Water misses little of the fun in life.

All three passages of the Grand Pitch must be portaged. The half-mile trail, which was badly overgrown until cleared by the Boy Scouts in 1975, begins eighty yards above the start of the rapids on the south (right) shore. At first, it follows Webster Brook, passing a possible campsite, then mounts an incline and proceeds inland around the falls, to which a short side path leads north (left). An evergreen clearing, which serves as a campsite, marks the place to return to the river. Continuing on the trail is unnecessary, for only an easy set of rips remains.

Worrying about his missing friend, Thoreau slept little that night. Rising early, he and Polis left Webster Brook without exploring the falls and walked three-quarters of a mile eastward through damp woods to the Penobscot's East Branch, down which they paddled to Grand Lake Matagamon.[4] Just below the Webster Brook inlet, they discovered Hoar camped on the southern shore. They celebrated their reunion over breakfast. This renowned place still provides rest for the weary. Slumber at the Little East Branch Lean-to. Behind this campsite is the Freezeout Trail, which continues eastward along an old tote (or lumbering) road to Trout Brook Farm (5.9 miles). Matagamon is only one-half mile farther—an uneventful ride, though shallow water can create some fast spots.

---

## Maine Woods Birds

### Great Blue Heron,
*Ardea herodias*

*How long we may have gazed on a particular scenery and think that we have seen and know it, when, at length, some bird or quadruped comes and takes possession of it before our eyes, and imparts to it a wholly new character. (August 14, 1859)*

One of Webster Brook's excitements is its wildlife. Unexpected creatures—moose, deer, beaver, and birds—can surprise you around any bend.

Canoeing downstream on August 22, 1979, we spied a great blue heron standing stately on a shoal. In the sunlight, his posture, color, and texture could have been mistaken for

Great blue heron

*A great blue heron at Baxter State Park*

driftwood stuck in the sand—a motionless, vertical statue of Aztec art. Since he appeared to be sleeping or posing for a portrait, we honored him with complete silence and several photographs. Nothing was audible except my pounding heart. We drifted within twenty yards, when he awoke. Giant wings expanded and gangling legs dangled in the air. He flew low over the water to the next point, where he again napped until we approached. This act was repeated countless times for the next three miles, until we stopped to camp at the Indian Carry Lean-to.

Thoreau saw only one great blue heron in Maine. His heron "winged its way slowly down the" Penobscot River below Piacataquis Falls. (293)

**Common Merganser,** *Mergus merganser*—**sheldrake or goosander**

"A long line of sheldrake, half grown, came waddling over" Webster Dam, interrupting Thoreau's dinner. (248) They played zestfully before his eyes, as they did at this exact spot thirty-one years later for Fannie Hardy Eckstorm, who watched them sail down through the sluice of the dam. As he proceeded down Webster Brook, Thoreau again observed:

*. . . a long string of sheldrakes, which something scared, run up the opposite side of the stream by me, with the same ease that they commonly did down it, just touching the surface of the waves, and getting an impulse from them as they flowed from under them. . . . (250)*

Neither the location nor behavior of twentieth-century sheldrakes has changed. They still display similar antics on Webster Brook. As our canoes and thoughts drifted with the current, twenty hazel eyes peered at us from the alders. Their unkempt hair matched the unkempt littoral. Silent swimmers stopped. Wings splashed droplets, then a row of iridescent spray, as the sheldrakes planed across the surface, their staccato movements startling us. This momentary

*Male common merganser*

*The spruce and fir trees crowded to the track on each side to welcome us, the* arbor-vitae *with
its changing leaves prompted us to make haste, and the sight of the canoe birch gave us spirits to do so. (93)*

CHAPTER 7

# Grand Lake Matagamon

Grand Lake Matagamon is a welcome change after Webster Brook—no falls, no rapids, no portages, and it is to be hoped, no headwinds. Just eight and a half miles of smooth paddling, this cruise was not the same when made by Thoreau as it is today. Thoreau passed through a pair of lakes: the larger in the east was called Matagamon (Thoreau's *Matungamook*), the Indian explanation of which was "old, second-class lake;" and, its smaller mate, Matagamonsis.[1] The two were linked by a two-mile-long morass, which Thoreau negotiated slowly:[2]

> *We continued along the outlet toward Grand Lake through a swampy region, by a long winding and narrow dead water, very much choked up by wood, where we were obliged to land sometimes in order to get the canoe over a log. It was hard to find any channel and we did not know but we should be lost in the swamp. (267–268)*

A larger dam has caused the flooding of this connection and the creation of one lake, which is actually a further expansion of the East Branch, which flows through this basin from its source, East Branch Pond, to its end, the Penobscot River.[3] Despite this difference, the voyage still has a fluvial flavor, especially when water is low enough to expose the former corridor.

## Trout Brook Farm

Close to where the swamp joined the larger lake, Thoreau passed the mouth of Trout Brook. Had he gone up this shallow stream for a mile an a half, he would have come to Trout Brook Farm, a popular grocery and hostel for lumberers and itinerants of his day. Fanny Hardy Eckstorm, who visited here on September 7, 1888, described the settlement:

> *The farm is mostly in mowing land, has some grain, and considerable hillside pasture. There are quite a number of buildings—barns, sheds and storehouses, and a low one story house with two rooms and a leanto several steps below.*

Today Trout Brook Farm is a campground within Baxter State Park. Reservations are required. Most people now come here by automobile; a few, by canoe or foot over Mataga-

Webster Brook

Second Lake

Freezeout Trail

1857

Mountain Catcher Pond

Dinner 30 July 1857

Thoreau Island

Grand Lake Matagamon

First Lake

Trout Brook Farm

Wadleigh Mountain

Trout Brook

Trout Brook Mountain

High Pond

Round Pond

Horse Mountain

Grand Lake Dam

The Crossing

Lower Fowler Pond

Long Pond

Billfish Pond

Billfish Mountain

Middle Fowler Pond

East Branch Penobscot

Campsite

Lower South Branch Pond

North Traveler Mountain

Bald Mountain

Black Cat Mountain

Upper South Branch Pond

Traveler Mountain

The Traveler

0      1      2      3 Miles

0    1    2    3    4  Kilometers

Method of Travel
——— Canoe or Bateau

mon or park trails. Robert N. Haskell recalled for me his first journey to Trout Brook Farm in 1928: he drove his car to Shin Pond; at sunrise he started walking the tote road, which took him sixteen miles to Matagamon; he crossed the lake in a scow and hiked along Trout Brook, reaching his lodgings at dusk.[4]

## Thoreau Island

*We stopped to dine on an interesting high rocky island soon after entering Matungamook lake, securing our canoe to the cliffy shore. (268)*

While on their spring drives, lumbermen performed a necessary task here. They kindled a fire, threw their winter clothes into the flames, and watched them turn to ash. They dubbed this place Louse Island, after the pest whose presence this ritual sought to eliminate. As a wooden sign testified, the name is now Thoreau Island in commemoration of Henry's fried-moose dinner here on July 30, 1857.[5] The island is privately owned and camping is not permitted, though you may bathe, botanize (see following natural history section), and meditate on the lake's serenity from a perch on the east end.

## Grand Lake Dam

*Here was a considerable fall, and a very substantial dam, but no sign of a cabin or camp. (271)*

The outlet of Matagamon is still marked by a fall and a dam, though not the 1847 dam that Thoreau described. The present concrete structure was built in 1940. Like Telos and Lock dams, it is owned by the East Branch Improvement Company of Bangor Hydro-Electric. A residence for the caretakers now stands here also.

To portage around the dam, follow the road past the home for about 200 yards. Turn left onto a path which leads to the East Branch. Polis entered the river here, while Thoreau and Hoar walked along the shore for a mile or more. If you wish to avoid the rapids below the dam, you may continue on the road until it joins Grand Lake Road, half a mile farther. Here there is a bridge across the river, a store, and a private campground.

## Additional Places of Interest

### "DEAD-WATER MOUNTAINS"

The beauty of the lake is enhanced by a group of hills lining its southern border. Polis referred to them as *Nerlumskeechticook* or "Dead-Water Mountains."[6] (270) They are now recognized individually as Wadleigh, Trout Brook, Horse, Billfish, and The Traveler. The latter, then called Carbuncle, was the only one identified on Thoreau's map.

This region, now within Baxter State Park, invites leisurely exploration. Two hikes excited me enough to repeat them several times. Both go from Matagamon to mountaintops for an overview of Thoreau country. The ascent of Horse Mountain is such a short trip that it fits into any schedule.

### NORTH TRAVELER (3,144 FEET)

Traveler Mountain, whose reputation for staying in view of East Branch canoeists earned it its name, is the celebrated feature of this landscape. North Traveler is its northernmost, but not its highest, peak.

Trout Brook Farm, 1.5 miles up Trout Brook from Matagamon, provides a base camp from which to see the surrounding area. To reach the summit of North Traveler and return here is more than a day's trip, so plan to spend one night at least at South Branch Pond Campground (reservations required).

From Trout Brook Farm, follow Park Tote Road west along Trout Brook for 4.7 miles to the Trout Brook Crossing (climbing 80 feet). (One mile west of Trout Brook Farm on this road, Five Ponds Trail leads south to a series of secluded ponds—the Fowlers, High, Long, Round, and Billfish. An esker divides High and Long Ponds.) At Trout Brook Crossing, turn south (left) and take the road to South Branch Ponds, 2.3 miles distant. A 2.7-mile trail leads from the campground there along the north ridge to the summit of North Traveler. Allow five to six hours for this complete trip.

### HORSE MOUNTAIN (1,589 FEET)

Horse Mountain fronts the western side of Matagamon's southernmost bay. To reach its summit from the lake is a 4.3-mile walk which averages two hours.

*White spruce*

Photo by Ben Kimball for the NH Natural Heritage Bureau

Dock your canoe at the marina for the High Adventure Program of the Boy Scouts of America, one mile north of Grand Lake Dam on the lake's west shore. Walk north along Park Tote Road, stopping at the Matagamon Gate of Baxter State Park to register (no fee for hikers). Continue on this road .6 mile to where a sign marks the start of the Horse Mountain Trail. This trail departs from the south (left) side of the road, and leads 1.4 miles to the top (796-foot climb), where an abandoned fire tower offers observation opportunities.

---

## Maine Woods Trees

The boreal forest dominates the landscape of Thoreau's travels north of Medway. The North Woods are immense. In Maine alone they cover over 15,000 square miles, or almost the northern half of the state. Beyond New England they proliferate, sweepng across Canada eastward to Newfoundland and westward to Alaska—and proceeding around the world south of the tundra. My biologist friends call it a "spruce-fir biome," which designates its most characteristic residents. Three species of spruce and one of fir are native to Maine. These evergreens are by no means its only tenants, however. Larch, arbor vitae, hemlock, and pine, as well as maple, aspen, alder, birch, and others, also live here. This country is, in fact, a good place to meet a variety of trees, as Thoreau did; he identified twenty-three species.

**Black Spruce,** *Picea mariana,* **White Spruce,** *Picea glauca,* **and Basalm Fir,** *Abies balsamea*

*My eyes were all the while on the trees, distinguishing between the black and white spruce and the fir. (108)*

When canoeing downstream, as Thoreau was, these conifers are

*Black spruce*

Photo by Ben Kimball for the NH Natural Heritage Bureau

not easy to tell apart. At a distance they appear alike—the same Christmas-tree foliage and profile. Upon closer inspection, differences emerge. The cones of the fir stand upright; those of the spruce hang down. Remove their needles. A small peg remains on the spruce twig, while that of the fir is flat.

The two spruces are also similar. Thoreau confused them for years. Polis, however, was able to recognize them quickly, either by sight or by touch. Black spruce, he explained, felt coarse in his hand, its needles being erect, while the reclining leaves of white spruce seemed softer. In general, the white spruce is a taller tree with longer needles and cones than the black; its twigs are smooth, while those of the black have minute hairs; and the color of its bark is lighter. These trees also prefer more diverse habitats. The black spruce enjoys bogs and mountains; it appears in its dwarf state near timberline on Katahdin. Masses of white spruce encompass lakes and streams and cover uplands.

Red spruce, *Picea rubens*, also dwells in this forest, though its

*White pine*

range, unlike that of its relatives, is limited to the eastern part of the continent. The question arises as to why Thoreau did not see this species. The answer is certainly that he did, but thought it a variety of the others since the botanies of his day did not classify it separately.[7]

*In short, though it looked very easy, I found that there was a great art in splitting these roots. (204)*

Polis used black spruce roots as thread to sew his birchbark canoes. He rejected white spruce for this purpose, complaining that they were "No good, break, can't split 'em." (188) Besides being stronger, the roots of black spruce were easier to obtain, since they grew closer to the surface than those of the white. Polis demonstrated his art for his companions. Digging a black spruce root, he split it in half with his knife, debarked each segment, and produced "a very neat, tough, and flexible string." (204)

*Red pine*

Spruces and firs served other functions as well. With their resins, the Indians pitched the outside seams and ends of their canoes, and mended rents in the birch-bark that occurred while traveling. When in dire need of food, they ate the inner bark of these trees. Gum was also made from black spruce. Today lumber companies grind up these woods for paper. Many are also sold for Christmas trees, the fir being superior since it holds needles longer.

## Northeastern Pine Forest

*Is it the lumberman then who is the friend and lover of the pine—stands nearest to it and understands its nature best? . . . No! no! it is the poet . . . who makes the truest use of the pine . . . who loves them as his own shadow in the air, and lets them stand. (121–122)*

Three species of pine—white, red, and jack—live in the great North Woods.[8] Thoreau met them all while in Maine, as you still can to-day. They are numerous and friendly. Thoreau Island is, in fact, a good place to get acquainted, since within this small space the triumvirate resides. In order to be properly introduced, you need to know who's who. White pine is the only pine in the East with five needles in a bundle; red and jack both have two needles, but the latter's are shorter—$^3/_4$ to $1^1/_2$ inches—the shortest in New England.

**White Pine,** *Pinus Strobus*—state tree of Maine; the white pine cone and tassel is the state's flower.

*I had come all this distance partly to see where the white-pine, the Eastern stuff of which our houses are built, grew, but . . . I had found it a scarce tree . . . (144)*

Down East Thoreau expected to witness the ultimate expression of the white pine. He wanted to behold pumpkin pines, those of exceptional age and wood, like the venerable one that lumberman John Springer felled—144 feet tall, six feet in diameter at four feet above the ground, and 65 feet without limbs—or to eye "a large community of pines, which had never been invaded by the lumbering army." (210) His search was disappointing. By the 1850s most of the virgin white pines were gone. They went to serve innumerable purposes, among which were construction of masts and hulls of sailing ships, doors, floors and panels of Yankee farms, bobsleds, and covered bridges. Their absence was particularly noticeable along the river banks, from whence they were most readily secured and transported to the mills. Beside the Penobscot stragglers and stumps of white pine remained, reminding Thoreau that their era had ended. Four years after his last tour, in 1861, the spruce harvest exceeded that of pine for the first time in Maine's history.

The demise of the white pine saddened Thoreau. He wanted it alive, not dead. Why, he wondered, do "so few ever come to the woods to see how the pine lives . . . to see its perfect success . . . "? He observed that:

*. . . the pine is no more lumber than man is, and to be made into boards and houses is no more its true and highest use than the truest use of man is to be cut down and made into manure. (121)*

*Jack pine*

To know the white pine, Thoreau might well have stayed at home, for in Concord they grew abundantly. He saw more of them there than in all of his Maine excursions. There he discovered their "concealed wildness," a new feature to botanists. Try for yourself these experiments. Take a pine needle in your hand. How many sides does it have? Move the needles across your lips in both directions. What do you feel? Thoreau found each of its leaves were "notched or serrated with minute forward-pointing bristles." (September 25, 1859) Why do you suppose nature designed them this way?

Massachusetts, not Maine, also provided Thoreau with his grandest stand of white pines. He came upon them while walking south from the New Hampshire border to Winchendon. They were part of a primitive forest along the railroad. More than their colossal size, "their perfect perpendicularity, roundness, and apparent smoothness, tapering very little, like artificial columns of a new style" impressed Thoreau. (June 4, 1858)

Besides beauty and lumber, pines also offer food and medicine. Their seeds, raw or roasted, are "sweet and nutritious," according to Fernald, who advises collecting them in August in order to minimize their resinousness. Even then, though, do not expect them to compare with the delicious pinyon nuts of the western pines. The young white pine shoots, boiled until tender and simmered in a sugar syrup, make a natural candy. Indians gathered the inner bark (cambium) to prepare a bread, with demand for it sufficient to leave the landscape marred by unclothed pineries. Euell Gibbons found white pine flour distasteful, and decided in the future to bake his rolls without it. Whatever you think of the flavor, be comforted in knowing that the bark is healthful, containing sugar, starch, and vitamin C. Its medicinal value is as an expectorant and a diuretic. It is still used as an ingredient in cough remedies.

**Red Pine,** *Pinus resinosa*

*We landed on a rocky point on the northeast side, to look at some Red Pines* (Pinus resinosa), *the first we had noticed, and get some cones, for our few which grow in Concord do not bear any. (243)*

These red pines stood on the shores of Telos Lake. Thoreau also found them growing on Thoreau Island and at Meadow Brook Rips below Grindstone on the Penobscot's East Branch. Red pines still thrive in these three stations, as well as elsewhere along Thoreau's itinerary. Unlike white pines, red pines appeared to him more often in the North Woods than in Concord, where as an indigenous species they were rare. Not until February 27, 1851, did he locate one in his hometown.

The English colonists of North American gave the red pine its other common first name. They mistook the tree for Norway spruce, which was exported from Scandinavia to Britain as lumber; however, the English apparently had not learned to identify the living tree from which the wood came. This misnomer has persisted for so long that its usage is now acceptable in all botanies. Thoreau frequently speaks of the trees as Norway pines.

**Jack Pine,** *Pinus Banksiana*—Rare and Endangered Species

*A peculiar evergreen overhung our fire which at first glance looked like a pitch pine* (P. rigida) *with leaves little more than an inch long—spruce-like; but we found it to be the "Pinus Banksiana—Banks' or the Labrador Pine" also called Scrub Pine, Grey Pine &c., a new tree to us. (268)*

Thoreau made this discovery on Thoreau Island in Grand Lake Matagamon on July 30, 1857. You can imagine his excitement over finding a species new to him. These conifers do not inhabit Concord, whose climate is too mild for them. Instead they prefer colder regions. They live farther north than any other American pine, growing to the edge of the Arctic Circle in Canada's Northwest Territories. Their capacity to endure nature's harshest elements is indeed laudatory.

Other nineteenth-century travelers located gray pines on Matagamon, though Thoreau's is the first record of its being there that I am aware of. They appeared on an unidentified island, which could have been Thoreau Island, to botanist George L. Goodale of the Maine Scientific Survey in late August 1861. A few days earlier upon Traveler Mountain he had added this tree to his "life-list" for the first time. In October 1882, George H. Witherle noticed them at his mainland campsite on Second Lake, as well as on several islands. The next fall on his way to Katahdin, he met jacks again, this time on the shore of Ambajejus Lake.[9] On September 7, 1888, Mrs. Eckstorm stopped specially on Louse Island for "a sprig of the Bank's Pine."

Lumbermen knew of the existence of gray pines on Matagamon before Thoreau. They left them alone, however, in favor of the white pine, whose size and wood was superior. As the white pine vanished, jacks were cut to fill many needs.[10] The loggers called them "shore" or "rock" pines, denoting their familiar habitat. Not wanting to be overshadowed, these evergreens delight in being by themselves, even though this means living in poorer soils.

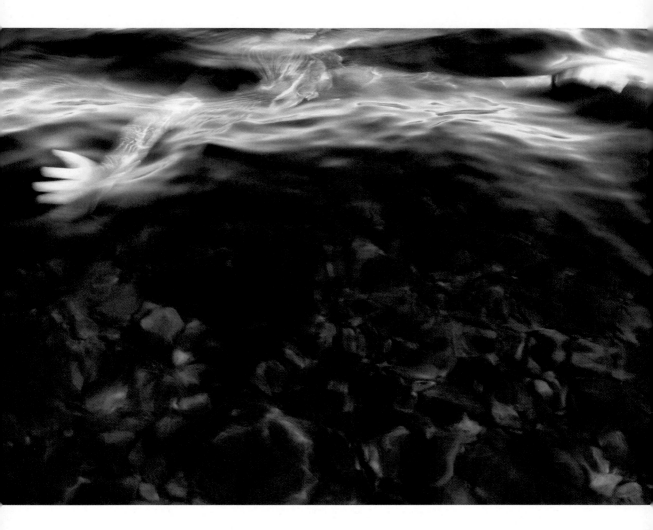

*We behold those features which the discoverers saw, apparently unchanged. (84)*

## CHAPTER 8
# East Branch of the Penobscot

## Grand Lake Matagamon to Hunt's Farm, 24 Miles

The East Branch, like the West Branch, was a logging river in Thoreau's time. It continued to serve that purpose for over one hundred years after Thoreau left. The annual cut, collected in Matagamon, was run down the East Branch to Medway, and from there, with the West Branch drive, went down the Penobscot to be milled and shipped at Bangor. In the twentieth century the trees stopped at Grindstone above Medway, and were transported overland to West Branch mills. Matagamon's reservoir and spring's freshets provided the power to advance the logs, while pickpoles, wing dams, and logan booms* kept them moving. Even with this assistance the ride was not easy. The river descended 408 feet in its 47.5 miles, averaging 8.6 feet per mile, and numerous falls and rapids jammed the loads, scattering logs in every direction.

No logs travel this way today. Except for tote roads, evidence of the river's former role has disappeared. Now when you step ashore in August, scarlet blooms of cardinal flowers, *Lobelia cardinalis,* cause you to stop in admiration. These red flames, long spikes which touch your knees, enliven this streambank dominated by browns, greens, and grays. My first association with the East Branch comes from this plant. Privately, I call it Cardinal Flower River.

In the past the East Branch has had other names. Polis applied *Wassataquoik* or "salmon" to the entire river. (283) A twenty-six-mile tributary, which enters from the west one mile above Hunt's Farm, retains this name. Fannie Hardy Eckstorm believed that the old Indian name (which she spelled *Wassategwewick*) referred only to the river's lower section. According to her, its meaning was "fish-spearing river," which is related to Polis's translation, for the speared species was the same.[1] Geologist Charles Hitchcock, who in 1861 ascended the East Branch, decided that it should have its own identity. He proposed that "Matagamon" be adopted as its name; others of that period, including Charles Hamlin, accepted this proposal.

*It is surprising on stepping ashore anywhere into this unbroken wilderness to see so often, at least within a few rods of the river, the marks of the axe, made by lumberers who have either camped here, or driven logs past in previous springs. (273)*

---

* A pickpole is a long pole with a spike on the end used for maneuvering and unjamming logs. A wing dam is a temporary dam built on top of a permanent dam to allow for the buildup of an extra-high head of water or to prevent water from circumventing the permanent dam. A logan boom is a boom, or chain, of logs surrounding or holding back the logs being driven. It is found in the many deadwaters, or logans, of Maine.

moved on to the mountain. J. K. Laski, who accompanied botanist Aaron Young Jr. here in 1847, added more details. Besides the main house, there were other "out buildings" and a large barn capable of holding several teams of oxen. One hundred acres of the 175-acre farm were cleared and planted with potatoes, oats, and hay; 75 tons of the latter were harvested in 1847. The produce was sold to lumberers working in the region.[7] Evidently, the intervale was quite fertile, for even uncultivated plants thrived. Botanist Goodale discovered wild lettuce twelve feet high and blue joint grass waving over his head.[8]

The historic inn that comforted so many travelers and lumberers is gone. The site, however, is still known by the same name. Though the forest has reclaimed the field, the place is easily identified by a small house. Across the river Hunt Mountain, rising over 1,100 feet above the valley, has been named in memory of this wilderness family.

## Hunt's Farm to Medway, 23.5 Miles

> *Thinking of the rapids, he [Polis] said once or twice, that you wouldn't catch him to go East Branch again; but he did not by any means mean all that he said. (287)*

Their intended trip to Katahdin aborted, the trio resumed paddling down the East Branch. Assuredly, Hoar was relieved at avoiding the arduous overland journey to the mountain. Their walking for the remainder of the trip was negligible. Thoreau mentions only two more carries on the East Branch. The first of these he called Whetstone Falls, which, judging by the distance he went, is today's Grindstone Falls. The old portage followed the west bank for three-quarters of a mile; late in the century a new path on the east side replaced it.

The location is important, for this was the scene of the Polis-Thoreau footrace—one of those rare moments in Thoreau's life when he ran . . . and won. While Polis, who proposed the contest, carried the greater weight, in the form of the canoe, Thoreau with "gun, axe, paddle, kettle, frying-pan, plates, dippers, carpets, & C.," had the more awkward load. For a handicap, Polis tossed his cowhide boots to the author, who was still packing, and departed. Unaccustomed as he was to such sport, Thoreau nevertheless overtook his rival. Before he could congratulate himself on his speed, his baggage dispersed in all directions. The outcome seemed decided. As Thoreau collected the strewn equipment, Polis sped by. Yet the seer of Walden, we find, was a strong competitor. Once engaged, he did not yield. With wares again bundled, he sprinted after his adversary, gained the lead, and this time held it. They finished out of breath and happy. Polis laughed, "O, me love to play sometimes." Thoreau agreed. Their second portage at Meadow Brook Rips was uneventful.

The twentieth-century passage is similar to that of Thoreau's time. With the possible exception of Grindstone Falls, you have the option of running all of the rapids. Lower water requires your carrying more frequently, or at least wading alongside your canoe to avoid injuring its bottom.

**East Branch—Lower Section; Hunt's Farm to Medway**

| Southbound Cumulative Mileage | Features | Description |
|---|---|---|
| 24.00 | Hunt's Farm | |
| 26.00 | Whetstone Falls 11 ft. in .4 mi. | Can be run successfully; on the east (left) bank is an MFS campsite preceding a bridge across the river |
| 34.50 | Hay Brook | Route 11 follows the river from here to Medway |
| 36.20 | Crowfoot Rapids 2 ft. in .1 mi. | Runnable |
| 38.10 | Grindstone Falls 30 ft. in 1.1. mi. | Picnic areas on east (left) bank at head and foot of rapids—no camping permitted—provide good places to begin and end the portage, which goes along the highway for one mile; rapids can be run with care and sufficient water, though carrying packs over the portage is recommended to reduce the load in the canoe |
| 40.10 | Meadow Brook Rips 7 ft. in .3 mi. | Formerly called Rocky Rips; easily run; a private campsite is located on the east (left) bank about forty minutes below this rapid |
| 45.10 | Ledge Falls 6 ft. in .3 mi. | Can be run with care |
| 47.50 | Medway | East Branch joins with West Branch to form Penobscot River |

## MEDWAY

> *Things are quite changed since I was here eleven years ago. Where there were but one or two houses, I now found quite a village, with saw-mills and a store . . . and there was a stage-road to Mattawamkeag, and the rumor of a stage. (287)*

At Medway—where Thoreau again unsuccessfully sought sugar—his East Branch excursion ended. Here the East Branch quietly melds with the West Branch to become the Penobscot River. This meeting place was known as *Nicatow*, meaning "fork of a river," and indicating its division into two branches.[9] The settlement on the north shore was known by this Indian name until 1875, when incorporation as a town caused it to be changed to Medway, designating its geographical position equidistant between Bangor and the northern part of Penobscot County. The Indian heritage is preserved in the name of the island at the confluence, Nicatow, which is still owned by the Penobscot Nation.

On Thoreau's earlier visit, September 3, 1846, his party called at the home of Benjamin Fiske, which was located on the shore opposite Nicatow Island. From there they

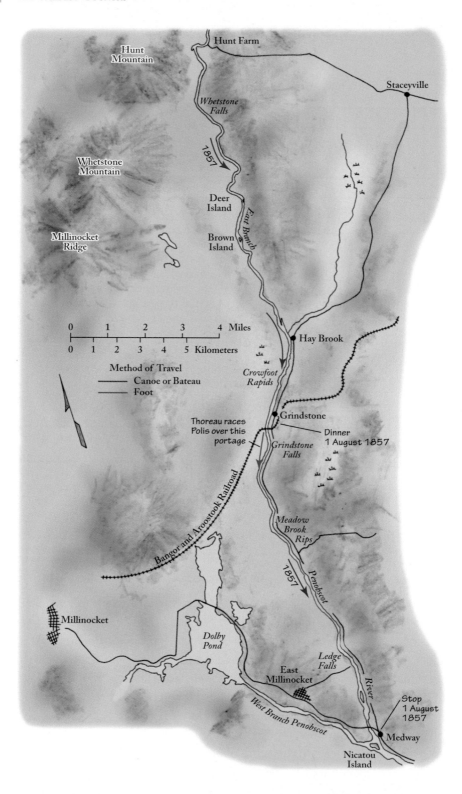

Hunt
Mountain

Hunt Farm

Staceyville

*Whetstone
Falls*

*1857*

Whetstone
Mountain

Deer
Island

*East Branch*

Brown
Island

Millinocket
Ridge

Hay Brook

0     1     2     3     4   Miles
0   1   2   3   4   5   Kilometers

Method of Travel
——— Canoe or Bateau
—— Foot

*Crowfoot
Rapids*

Grindstone

Thoreau races
Polis over this
portage

Dinner
1 August 1857

*Grindstone
Falls*

*Meadow
Brook
Rips*

*Bangor and Aroostook Railroad*

*1857*

*Penobscot*

Millinocket

*Dolby
Pond*

*Ledge
Falls*

East
Millinocket

*River*

Stop
1 August
1857

*West Branch Penobscot*

Medway

Nicatou
Island

obtained passage across the river, where they began walking up the south side of the West Branch on their way to Katahdin. Unfortunately, the lovely Fiske home, which after Thoreau's appearance was expanded and became the town's hotel, was demolished in the late 1960s. One of Thoreau's West Branch guides, George McCauslin, is buried at Medway's Lynch Cemetery.[10]

At Medway, a choice of destinations exists. You may descend the Penobscot River to Old Town and Bangor, thereby completing Thoreau's 1857 trip. This is described in Chapter 11. Or, the West Branch can be ascended to the foot of Katahdin, as Thoreau did in 1846. The next chapter narrates this adventure. The former journey, while longer, is more relaxed, since you proceed with the current and without so many obstacles. However, approaching Katahdin on the West Branch across the lakes above the North Twin Dam is one of life's special moments.

*Belted kingfisher*

## Maine Woods Birds

**Belted Kingfisher,** *Megaceryle alcyon*

*We had smooth but swift water for a considerable distance, where we glided rapidly along, scaring up ducks and kingfishers. (276)*

Thus commenced Thoreau's second day on the East Branch. Kingfishers must have made him feel at home, for they were part of his Concord landscape as well. At home he had observed them often as he boated on the Assabet River.

As you descend the East Branch in the summer, kingfishers certainly will be there. They take great pride in this valley and constantly attend to its welfare. They are the inspectors of its water quality and shoreline beauty, the trustees of its natural heritage.

They depend upon it for survival.

Their cuisine is in its currents. From the air they spot fish swimming, and dive to catch them in their large bills, which remind me of trumpet mutes, though this is perhaps an unfair exaggeration.

Their nests are in its banks. They excavate long, horizontal tunnels into sand and gravel with terminal chambers for their eggs. Both sexes create the lair and then incubate and feed the young.

When I went this way the kingfishers were silent. Their alarm, a rattling yell—a "most unmusical note," Thoreau remarked (April 25, 1852)—went unsounded as my group passed. They were not fishing either, just staring at us from atop aerial spires where they perched. But then, as if on cue, their circus performance began. Like trapeze artists, they swung from one side of the river to the other, only the exercise was performed without ropes. They flew back and forth just below the treetops, moving downstream as they crossed. What fun they have in life! Their serious demeanor is misleading. Like loons and mergansers, they enjoy a frolic each day.

# Maine Woods Fruits

*I have added a few to my number of edible berries by walking behind an Indian in Maine, who ate such as I never thought of tasting before. Of course they made a much greater account of wild fruits than we do. (January 8, 1861)*

*Blueberries*

In such a manner Thoreau learned about Maine's esculents. We can only wish that we knew all of the kinds that he sampled. His narrative mentions only a few; these are presented below. By reading his flora list, however, we can surmise others that he tried: strawberries, cherries, elderberries, and even the bland and mealy bearberries.

### Blueberries, *Vaccinium* **spp., and Raspberries,** *Rubus* **spp.**

*There was not a carry on the main East Branch where we did not find an abundance of both these berries....Another name for making a portage would have been going a berrying. (277)*

Foraging for edibles enhances the pleasure of walking. Even if you have tasted the cultivated varieties, eating them wild is an entirely new experience. Their presence increases your load but stimulates your step.

Little need be said of these common perennials other than to remind you to keep an eye out for them. These fruits seem to be everywhere. They prefer regenerating disturbed areas, sandy and sunny fields, or sides of lumber roads; raspberries in particular like a little moisture in their world.

Habitats of blueberries vary from bogs and swamps, where the highbush, *V. corymbosum,* grows, to mountaintops, where you will find the low and sweet variety, *V. angustifolium.* Thoreau nibbled blueberries all the way up Katahdin, discovering that altitude improved their flavor. (66) He called them ambrosia, fruits of the gods. (July 29, 1853) The Penobscots also relished these delicious berries. Hot blueberry bread was a favorite recipe. By drying blueberries and raspberries, they could enjoy them year-round. Thoreau's enthusiasm encompassed both their digestion and their fragrance: "It is so much more desirable at this season to breathe the raspberry air of Maine." (August 3, 1857)

*Juneberries*

*Generally speaking, a howling wilderness does not howl;*
*it is the imagination of the traveler that does the howling. (219)*

### CHAPTER 9

# West Branch of the Penobscot,
## Southern Section

## Medway to Elbow Lake, 14 Miles

From Medway the West Branch led Thoreau to and from Katahdin. It was not an easy journey in either direction. The Indians knew well the effort required to go upstream. Imagine their infuriation with the settlers, who not only despoiled their land but changed the course of the rivers! Thoreau found the descent equally demanding and far more dangerous. (73) Though he had done some boating before, nothing compared with the West Branch.

Actually, Thoreau did not enter the river immediately. Except for a row on Millinocket Stream and across Quakish Lake, he waited until Elbow Lake before beginning his trip. I would recommend doing likewise. By beginning your voyage there or at North Twin Lake, which is accessible by road, you avoid the modern complications of pulpwood, paper mills, and dams, none of which (except North Twin Dam) impeded Thoreau's progress. Should you wish to canoe this section of the river, as I have done twice, be prepared for opposition.

### GEORGE MCCAUSLIN'S FARM

> *In fact, the deeper you penetrate into the woods, the more intelligent, and, in one sense, less countrified do you find the inhabitants; for always the pioneer has been a traveler, and, to some extent, a man of the world. . . . (22)*

On September 3, 1846, Thoreau, George Thatcher, and the latter's two Bangor friends reached Medway on foot from Mattawamkeag.[1] After crossing to the south shore there, the pedestrians followed a faint trail along the West Branch, passing several rapids. Four and one-half miles from the fork between the East and West branches, they stopped opposite George McCauslin's farm, which stood at the mouth of Schoodic Stream, on its west bank.[2] Here they were ferried across the West Branch. Today this ride to the river's north

> *The Indians say, that the river once ran both ways, one half up and the other down, but, that since the white man came, it all runs down, and now they must laboriously pole their canoes against the stream, and carry them over numerous portages (32–33)*

Katahdin Stream

Abol Stream

Return: 8 Sept. 1846 Boatmen carry baggage over portage, let bateau over falls

Abol Falls

Camp 6 Sept. 1846 Dinner 8 Sept. 1846

Pockowockamus Falls

Greenville

Pockowockamus

Deadwater

Oak Hall Carry Camp: 8 Sept. 1846 Dinner 6 Sept. 1846

Debsconeag Falls

Millinocket

First Debsconeag Lake

Debsconeag Deadwater

Road

Going: 6 Sept. 1846 Thoreau and boatmen "warp up" Passamagamet Falls; others walk over baggage. Return: 9 Sept. 1846: boatmen run Passamagamet Falls; Thoreau walks around with baggage.

Millinocket Lake

Return: 9 Sept. 1846 Boatmen run Ambejejus Falls Thoreau carries baggage over

Breakfast 6 and 9 Sept.

Ambejejus Lake

Summer home of Frederic Edwin Church

Pemadumcook Lake

1846

Little Porus Island

Camp 5 Sept. 1846

Wadleigh Brook

Lower Jo-Mary Lake

North Twin Lake

Black Island

5 Sept. 1846 Logger's Camp Supper, portage over dam

Elbow Lake

1846

North Twin Dam

Quakish Lake

South Twin Lake

Return: 9 Sept. 1846 Boatmen use sluiceway while Thoreau portages

0    1    2    3    4 Miles
0  1  2  3  4  5 Kilometers

Method of Travel
——— Canoe or Bateau
——— Foot

shore is considerably longer. The West Branch, Schoodic Stream, and George McCauslin's property have been flooded by Dolby Pond, which was created by Dolby Dam completed in 1907 for water and pulp storage for Great Northern's mill at East Millinocket.

Thoreau lodged at McCauslin's three nights, two of them on his outward trip. He enjoyed his host's "Scotch hospitality . . . dry wit and shrewdness, and . . . general intelligence. . . ." McCauslin—Uncle George to his intimates—was fifty-two years old, "had been a waterman twenty-two years, and had driven the lakes and head waters of the Penobscot five or six springs in succession. . . . " (22) He was now farming for family and lumberers. Hay, potatoes, carrots, turnips, and corn grew in his fields.

## THE FOWLER FARMS

*"Those Fowler boys," said Mrs. McCauslin, "are perfect ducks for the water." (77)*

Thoreau and Thatcher persuaded Uncle George to lead them upriver, their Indian guides not having come as expected. They walked along the north bank of the West Branch over an obscure trail to the house of Thomas Fowler Jr. four miles west. Fowler's log cabin,

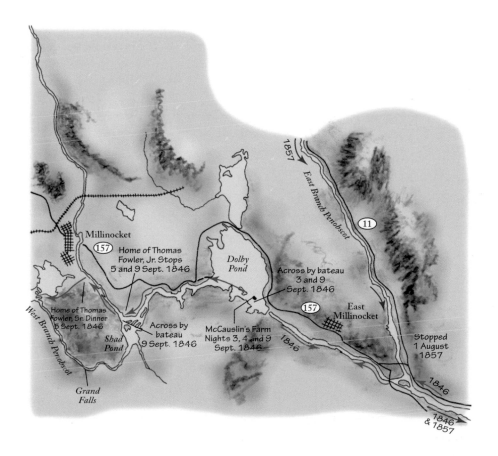

which was just being finished, was located on the east shore of Millinocket Stream at Shad Pond. George McCauslin was pleased to see his daughter, Aurora, who was Tom's wife. Over a draught of spruce beer, the twenty-four-year-old Fowler, an adept bateauman, accepted his visitors' invitation to join them. Donning boots and red flannel shirt, he was set for the wilderness.

From Fowler's, several courses were possible. The party could have taken Millinocket Stream eight miles to the lake of the same name, and from there portaged into Ambajejus Lake, thus returning to the West Branch. In September 1837, Charles Jackson

### West Branch: Medway to North Twin Dam Farm

| Northbound Cumulative Mileage | Mileage Between Features | Features | Description |
|:---:|:---:|:---:|:---|
| .00 | .00 | Medway Bridge, Route 116 | Junction of East and West branches. |
| .50 | .50 | Bangor Hydroelectric Dam | Portage on north (right) side on road, .1 mi. |
| 2.25 | 1.75 | GN mill, East Millinocket | Portage either side: north (right) on the road through mill; south (left) through bush to road which follows river. It is worthwhile carrying to Dolby Pond. |
| 4.00 | 1.75 | Dolby Dam | Portage on north (right) side on road past hydroelectric plant and boom; spectacular view of Katahdin. |
| 7.00 | 3.00 | Jerry Brook Rapids | Walk canoes through close to shore; slow going. |
| 8.50 | 1.50 | Millinocket Stream | Swift current can be navigated. |
| 10.00 | 1.50 | GN mill, Millinocket | Portage on west (left) on mill roads. |
| 10.50 | .50 | Ferguson Lake | May contain pulp and booms. |
| 11.50 | 1.00 | Quakish Lake Dam | Spillway on north (right) side can be navigated. |
| 13.50 | 2.00 | Quakish Thoroughfare | Swift current can be navigated. |
| 14.00 | .50 | North Twin Dam | Portage on north (right) side over rock pile to path to road; turn left and take road past dam and boom to Elbow Lake. Possible campsites en route. |

*The Grand Pitch on the West Branch of the Penobscot River in the 1930s*

went this way to Katahdin.[3] At the time, this route to the mountain was thought to be more direct than remaining with the West Branch; in reality, both routes to Ambajejus Lake are the same distance, 16.5 miles. Upper Millinocket Stream, according to Jackson, presented "several difficult and rocky rapids;" but those were much less intimidating than the deluge of the West Branch in the four miles between Shad Pond and Quakish Lake. Neither passage was pleasant. Thoreau's party rejected both in favor of a third alternative: a two-mile bypass around the worst of West Branch. This carry began at the home of Thomas Fowler Sr. one and a half miles up Millinocket Stream, which was ascended in a leaky bateau.

Canadian voyageurs prayed when passing a place on the river where someone had been killed. This old custom has been repeated many times on the West Branch, where in the line of duty lumbermen have often drowned. Before leaving Shad Pond, pay your respects to Joe Aitteon, Thoreau's 1853 guide and governor of the Penobscots. On July 4, 1870, he with six other log drivers upset their bateau in the rocky rapids above Grand Falls; four of them perished. After plunging over the cataract, Aitteon's 225-pound body came to rest in Shad Pond, where it was found six days later. Aitteon was forty, four years younger than Thoreau when he died.

In the late 1830s, the elder Fowler moved from south of Shad Pond to Millinocket Stream. He was attracted to the land by its potential to feed the lumberers, as well as by its strategic position for conveying their supplies around Grand Falls. The Indians had made a trail here which Fowler further developed. His improvements left something to be desired, however. Geologist James Hodge, arriving in June 1837, was one of his first customers. An ox-sled transported his bateau and baggage "over a rough hilly road, filled with boulders of granite and slate."[4] Nine years later, under different power, Thoreau found the terrain as formidable: "The route . . . was in some places the roughest ever travelled by horses, over rocky hills, where the sled bounced and slid along, like a vessel pitching in a storm." (30) Undaunted, Thoreau again went via Fowler's Carry on his return trip.

Despite its primitiveness, this portage was well used until the end of the century. Old Fowler died on his farm in 1874; his youngest son, Francis, remaining there for eight more years sold the property to his nephew, Charles T. Powers, who stayed until 1899, when the Great Northern Paper Company, which was formed as such that year, became the owner. The pastoral personality of the landscape vanished quickly. Great Northern, wishing to shorten the river drive and capitalize on the region's water power, built its mill in Fowler's front yard. On November 9, 1900, the first newsprint was manufactured here. The plant also produced the town of Millinocket around it; it incorporated the following year with 2,000 residents. A road was constructed up the West Branch from Medway along the trail blazed by the elder Fowler, and the Fowler home, where Thoreau stopped, became a boarding house and town's first post office.

The modern portage, while vastly different from the old, is equally challenging. With patience and fortitude, Fowler's Carry can still be partially retraced. I have never experienced a crossing quite like it, however. Coming up Millinocket Stream, we landed beside Great Northern's parking lot in the heat of the late afternoon of August 13, 1975. Laden with packs, paddles, and canoe, we weaved among the cars to the plant. As we approached, a security guard stopped us. I informed him that our mission was strictly academic; we were following the footsteps of Henry Thoreau as part of a course I was offering, and permission to trespass had been given by the company's public affairs manager, Paul McCann. The guard's confounded expression showed his disbelief. I imagined that his family would hear tonight of how he arrested the saboteurs who tried to infiltrate the plant in the guise of voyageurs. After a short delay, he let us by. We climbed a flight of stairs to the upper level, emerging between buildings. Here our path was well marked by two parallel white lines painted on the pavement, staying within which assured our safety from fork-lift trucks transporting pallets of paper. We stopped in the personnel office, not for employment, but for a drink of cold water, since we had not consumed any from the West Branch. Revived, we moved westward along a road which shortly intersected the railroad, and eventually reached Ferguson Lake where we could paddle. This lake, created in 1899, submerged the rest of Fowler's Carry, this making our haul shorter than Thoreau's.

A navigable spillway joins Ferguson and Quakish lakes. The latter affords an agreeable cruise until the strait, which still requires, as Thoreau remarked, "all the strength and skill of our boatmen to pole up it." (33) On the carry around North Twin Dam, Thoreau's

Courtesy of Special Collections, Raymond H. Fogler Library, University of Maine at Orono

*The grave of Joseph Aitteon on Indian Island, showing a spelling different from the one Thoreau used*

party had supper at a logger's camp. Returning from Katahdin, Fowler and McCauslin ran the sluice, not inhibited by a ten-foot drop. (76) Like all dams Thoreau saw, this "lofty and solid structure, with sloping piers some distance above, made of frames of logs filled with stones," has been improved since his visit. (34)

## Elbow Lake to Ambajejus Lake, 8.25 Miles

*The country is an archipelago of lakes,—the lake-country of New England. (36)*

Above North Twin Dam, the West Branch widens to form a series of exhilarating lakes— North and South Twin, Pemadumcook, Ambajejus. Traveling over them by day or night inspires music. In moonlight, Thoreau crossed North Twin Lake singing one of his favorite tunes, the "Canadian Boat Song":

*"Row, brothers, row, the stream runs fast,*
*The Rapids are near and the daylight's past!" (38)*

"A small island near the head of the lake," Black Island, guided them. (37) Beyond this beacon they camped on the north shore near Wadleigh Brook, having come five miles from the dam.

Actually, when entering North Twin Lake, Little Porus Island, two miles beyond Black Island, comes into view first. One year we paddled North Twin after sunset, finding Little Porus Island in the dark. With a tiny cove and white sand beach, this lovely isle is a welcome haven. Though not marked as an official campsite, it obviously has been used as such. The beach, coated with pine needles, makes a perfect bed; swimming is excellent. In all directions—north into Ambajejus, west across Pemadumcook, southeast over North Twin—there are marvelous panoramas. Except for the houses along Nicks Gut, the shores are as unsettled as those Thoreau witnessed: "There was the smoke of no log-hut nor camp of any kind to greet us. . . . " (36) An occasional motorboat runs from Spence Cove to Pemadumcook Lake; otherwise, serenity is the predominant mood.

Thoreau moved from North Twin across Pemadumcook into Ambajejus Lake. Thoroughfares or reaches of river connected these lakes. Since then these straits have disappeared. The lakes, whose elevations were raised by North Twin Dam, now blend together as one. Ambajejus appealed to Thoreau "as the most beautiful lake we had ever seen." (44) Hubbard's impression of Ambajejus changed after the new water level killed the surrounding vegetation. His *Guides* informed the adventurer of what to expect. At first, Ambajejus was "a pretty sheet of water some four miles long." (1879, p. 74) Later, he referred to it as "rather bleak and cheerless." (1893, p. 77) Now, with its lush and thriving shore, Ambajejus has regained its mid-nineteenth century reputation for beauty.

## MILLINOCKET LAKE: FREDERIC EDWIN CHURCH

A narrow strip of land separates Ambajejus and Millinocket lakes. Thoreau never walked across this isthmus or entered Millinocket Lake. The former solitude of this crossing is now lost to the animation of summer tourists motoring the Greenville-Millinocket Road, visiting the Millinocket Trading Post and Campground, or flying off in seaplanes.

Along Millinocket Lake's southern shore about 2.5 miles from the portage lies the old Stevens Farm, whose fields oxen once plowed. Frederic Edwin Church, one of America's renowned landscape painters, bought this property in 1878. Often during the ensuing summers and autumns, Church could be found here relaxing, fishing, or sketching one of his favorite subjects, Katahdin, which poses strikingly across the lake and forest. His last dated work, in fact, was of this sublime scene.

Church and Thoreau had much in common. As travelers, naturalists, artists, and mountain zealots, they were devoted to the North Woods. Each in his own idiom created a timeless interpretation of Katahdin. Each felt elevated by his Maine experiences, enough so to want them repeated and shared.[5] Church encouraged an old friend to

**West Branch: Ambajejus Lake to Abol Stream**

| Northbound Cumulative Mileage | Mileage Between Features | Features | Description |
|---|---|---|---|
| — | — | Ambajejus Lake, south end | |
| 2.50 | 2.50 | Ambajejus Falls | This thoroughfare can be paddled up. |
| 4.25 | 1.75 | Passamagamet Lake | To the west, below falls. |
| 4.50 | .25 | Passamagamet Falls | Portage on right (east) in north end of tiny cove, about ¼ mile. |
| 6.00 | 1.50 | Debsconeag Deadwater | |
| 8.00 | 2.00 | Debsconeag Falls | Portage on left (north), about ¼ mile. |
| 8.50 | .50 | Pockwockamus Deadwater | |
| 11.00 | 2.50 | Pockwockamus Falls | Portage on left (west) on road .3 mile around both sections. |
| 12.00 | 1.00 | Abol Falls | Portage on left (west) on road for .1 mile. |
| 12.75 | .75 | Abol Deadwater, mouth of Abol Stream | |

*go to the Maine Woods in the vicinity of Mt. Ktaadn with your fishing rod. It has a wonderful climate . . . and the trout are the finest in the world. I can tell you exactly where to go and the names of the guides[;] they are splendid fellows.*

*It is an easy trip too.*[6]

In 1898, two years before Church's death, his son Louis built a permanent residence at Millinocket Lake. Like his father, the younger man enjoyed the retreat, returning yearly for a month at a time until 1924. He and his guests arrived by boat from Norcross across North Twin and Ambajejus lakes.[7] His two-story log cabin with handsome stone fireplace and two small camps still occupies this site. Since 1958, Elmer R. Woodworth has owned the Church hermitage, which is now for sale. One winter he removed Church's solid-oak icebox, hauling it by sled across the snow. He gave it, along with a birch table and wood-stove, to Church's estate, Olana.

# Ambajejus Lake to Abol Stream, 12.75 Miles

From Ambajejus Lake to Abol Stream, the West Branch alternates between stretches of fast and slow current, between river and deadwater. The wayfarers stopped for breakfast at the north end of Ambajejus, at "the site of an old loggers' camp, remembered by McCauslin, now overgrown with weeds and bushes." (45) Their resting place, considering the new shoreline, was probably in the vicinity of the present Ambajejus Camps, which are leased to vacationers who motor here over the Millinocket-Greenville Road. A bridge crosses the river just above this retreat. Thoreau's party left the lake there and went upriver one-quarter mile to Ambajejus Falls; they surmounted the falls by carrying the bateau on padded shoulders while others steadied the craft and lugged the baggage. The falls having been inundated, the portage is no longer necessary, but the paddle is strenuous. With this exception, the contemporary river, described in the chart on the previous page, resembles what Thoreau experienced.

Fowler and McCauslin decided to "warp up"* their next obstacle, Passamagamet Falls. Their success was a first in West Branch history; Thoreau captured the drama:

> *With an uncertain and wavering motion we wound and bolted our way up, until the bow was actually raised two feet above the stern at the steepest pitch; and then, when everything depended upon his exertions, the bowman's pole snapped in two; but before he had time to take the spare one, which I reached him, he had saved himself with the fragment upon a rock; and so we got up by a hair's breadth; . . . (48–49)*

A clear trail bypasses Passamagamet Falls. On the return trip, Thoreau took it, while his guides again shot the rapids. Passamagamet Lake opens to the west before the cataract. Such a wilderness lake deserves at least one campsite, but our circumnavigation revealed none.

Impressed with the feat of his boatmen, Thoreau wanted to test his own skill. A half-mile above Passamagamet Falls, the West Branch turns sharply west, producing fast water through which canoes usually have to be waded even today. Thoreau attempted to pole past this rapid, "Thatcher's Rips" he called it in his notes. He almost succeeded when the bateau, hitting a rock, went spinning. The experts rescued the crew.

Shortly, Debsconeag Deadwater is reached—"One of the shallowest and weediest of the lakes," Thoreau observed, and it is still an apt description. (50) Drowned logs on the bottom can be seen from the surface. In the east bay, an inviting beach serves as a campsite and swimming area. Since a dirt road touches the shore there, so do many people and vehicles. (This road runs three miles to the Millinocket Road and takes about one hour to walk.) In 1976, six of us spent a quiet August night here by ourselves. The next day,

---

* Warping up involves tying a rope to something firm ashore—a rock or tree—to aid the boat's upstream movement. Thoreau put it thusly: "Leaping from rock to rock in the shoal water close to the shore, and now and then getting a bite with the rope round an upright one, I held the boat while one reset his pole, and then all three forced it upward against any rapid. This was 'warping up'." (52)

ATAHDIN FROM THE MOUTH OF ABOL ON THE PENOBSCOT WEST BRANCH.

Maine Historical Society

*View of Katahdin from the mouth of Abol Stream in 1900*

a division of Explorer Scouts rolled in, unpacked their trucks, and bivouacked. Forced to retreat before this horde of a hundred, we sought the solitude of First Debsconeag Lake, one mile west, which offers several resting places. My favorite lies near the entrance on the southern shore.

Above Debsconeag Deadwater, where the West Branch narrows and turns eastward, the current quickens and demands exertion for a short distance. A calm section precedes Debsconeag Falls. The trail around the falls, overgrown and not easily discernable at first, leads inland before changing directions to parallel the river. On September 6, Thoreau ate dinner on this carry and, two nights later when going downstream, slept here. (50, 75) He christened this portage "Oak Hall" for a famous men's clothing store of Boston, whose advertisement he saw stuck with pitch to a nearby pine. The Indians called the falls and lower deadwater *Katepsconegan*, which can be translated as "carrying place" and from which the present name, Debsconeag, is corrupted.

Katahdin makes a vivid impression on the traveler of the West Branch. It strikes its most sublime pose over the lakes, often doubling its solid image in their liquid surfaces. Ambajejus, Debsconeag, and Pockwockamus vie for the best photograph. Over their blue waters and green forests, the monolith dominates the horizon. Its weathered, ashen face and wrinkled, level brow gives the Penobscot Valley its distinction. A spectator of this scene, Thoreau withheld his reactions until he knew the mountain more intimately. Paddling Pockwockamus, we receive the temple's magic, and rejoice.

Beyond Pockwockamus Deadwater is the falls of the same name. The torrent, before which a sandy island provides a place to rest, is divided into two sections: Big, lower; Little, upper. It is best to carry both pitches at once. A dirt road along the river permits easy transit northward. If desired, it can be followed the rest of the way to Abol Stream, 1.5 miles. Or, you can return to the river above Little Pockwockamus and paddle one-half mile to Abol Falls, which along with the rapids above must be passed on the road; then navigate the swift water under Thoreau Bridge—it was dedicated to him on September 11, 1971—to the entrance of Abol Stream, where there is a public campground. A grocery store is available along the highway here, too.

Thoreau carried around Big Pockwockamus Falls, then warped up the next part while the men ashore carried the wangan, or baggage. The same portage-pole routine was repeated for Abol Falls and the rapid beyond. Camp was prepared at the mouth of two streams, Murch and Aboljacknagesic—now called Katahdin and Abol, respectively—on the Abol Deadwater (Thoreau's Sowadnehunk). Sowadnehunk now applies to the stretch of river four miles ahead.[8] Thoreau does not give his exact position. Whether he was situated between the two streams or south of Abol is a matter of conjecture.

---

## Maine Animals

### Eastern Woodland Caribou, *Rangifer tarandus caribou*

*. . . when I was walking over the carry, close behind the Indian, he observed a track on the rock, which was but slightly covered with soil, and, stooping, muttered "caribou." (278)*

Thoreau did not see any caribou in Maine. You are not even likely to find their footprints. These mammals, however, were a conspicuous feature in the North Woods of the nineteenth century. Many reports by travelers confirmed their presence. In the summer of 1820, American surveyors for the Maine Boundary Commission killed a caribou wandering along Chesuncook Lake; when dressed it weighed 200 pounds and, cooked, it tasted better than "beef and the common venison," they contended. Portaging between Millinocket and Ambajejus lakes on September 21, 1837, Jackson met a reindeer trotting along the shore, which, detecting the explorers, de-

*Eastern woodland caribou*

parted quickly without paying his respects. The same thing happened to Lucius L. Hubbard. While he was coasting down Lobster Stream in September 1881, a caribou approached him, then decided to retreat into the alders. On September 6, 1888, Fannie Hardy Eckstorm and her father watched another party attempt to blast two of the beasts off the surface of Hay Brook Logan of Grand Lake Matagamon; fortunately, their shots went astray. And, in February 1892, Lore Rogers counted eighteen caribou atop Katahdin. Apparently, their last authentic appearance was in 1908.

Their demise is regrettable. It plainly illustrates the consequences of not conserving our natural resources. Their loss, which is not yet fully understood, is attributed to several causes. Certainly one reason they left was their distaste for being shot at and for having their families destroyed, a sentiment easy to sympathize with. Indiscriminant killing of the creatures prevailed during the nineteenth century. Indians and whites hunted them for food, clothing, and trophies. Not until 1900, when most were gone, was their protection guaranteed by law. Even afterward, hunters persisted until the last few were finished off. Another explanation of their extirpation is the change in their environment wrought by homesteaders, lumbering, and forest fires.

Their last domain was Katahdin. Here they lived on the Tableland for nearly half the year. You might wonder what an animal of this size was doing on a plateau of this height for a period of this length? The answer is eating. Unlike moose, caribou migrate, changing their feeding ground with the seasons. In the summer, they grazed the woods around the mountain, enjoying the fresh, green leaves of deciduous trees, especially those of willows, birches, and blueberries. After the heavy frosts of autumn, they climbed Katahdin to indulge in their favorite repast: lichens. They found most palatable two varieties of fruticose lichens, *Cladonia rangiferina* and *Cladonia alpestris*, both of which are commonly called reindeer lichens after their principal consumers.

Although their fare is still ample on Katahdin, caribou have not returned—at least not voluntarily. If you were on Baxter Peak in December 1963, you would have witnessed an unexpected sight, though: a herd of caribou contentedly grazing on the tundra. Where did they come from? Lake Victoria, Newfoundland, some 600 miles distant. Their migration was mechanical, however. Captured while swimming the lake and then sedated, they were transported by truck to the base of Katahdin, from whence Navy jet helicopters lifted them onto the Tableland. They stayed in their new home until the beginning of April, when they journeyed down the mountain in search of different provender. Later surveys by the biologist in charge of the project, Francis Dunn, showed them dispersed throughout the Maine woods. They never returned to their former habitat and gradually decreased in abundance. In 1980, Dunn told me that, though their reintroduction had been a failure, "there might be an offspring of the original animals still around."

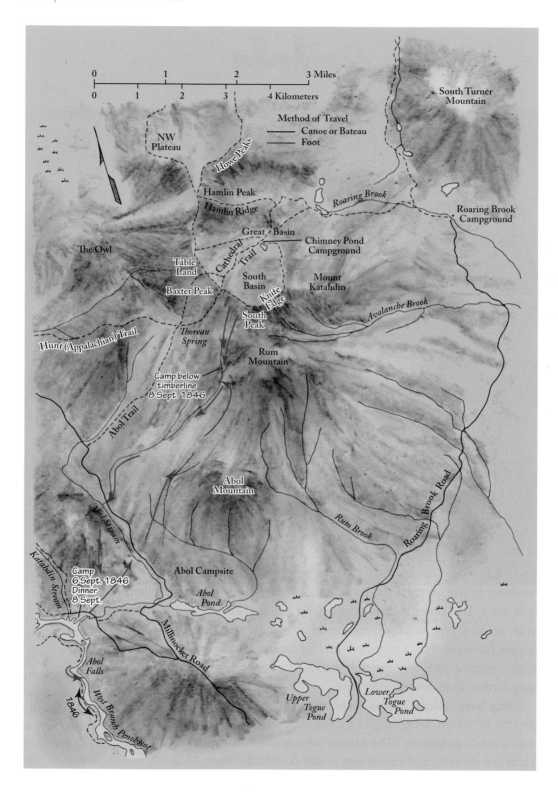

South Turner
Mountain

NW
Plateau

Howe Peaks

Hamlin Peak

Hamlin Ridge

Roaring Brook

Roaring Brook
Campground

The Owl

Great Basin

Chimney Pond
Campground

Table
Land

Cathedral Trail

South
Basin

Mount
Katahdin

Baxter Peak

Knife
Edge

South
Peak

Avalanche Brook

Thoreau
Spring

Hunt (Appalachian) Trail

Rum
Mountain

Camp below
timberline
8 Sept. 1846

Abol Trail

Abol
Mountain

Rum Brook

Roaring Brook Road

Abol Stream

Abol Campsite

Camp
6 Sept. 1846
Dinner
8 Sept.

Abol
Pond

Katahdin Stream

Millinocket Road

Upper
Togue
Pond

Lower
Togue
Pond

Abol
Falls

1846

West Branch Penobscot

0        1        2        3 Miles

0    1    2    3    4 Kilometers

Method of Travel
——— Canoe or Bateau
——— Foot

Slide and Tableland to the summit. She had pursued her own recommendation on August 20–21, 1889, commenting that "We made the ascent easily."[2] By the late nineteenth century, this had become the standard approach to the mountain from the West Branch, its being then marked by a rude trail and approved by Lucius Hubbard in his *Guides*.

It was also used by at least two of Thoreau's predecessors: Jacob Bailey in 1836 and Charles Jackson in 1837.[3] Both scientists probably did not decide their route themselves. They enlisted the aid of guides, who despite their being novices regarding Katahdin, nevertheless succeeded admirably. Bailey employed two loggers, both of whom were new to the mountain, to pilot him; they selected Abol Slide and attained the summit, though Bailey himself stopped short of the Tableland. Jackson's escort was the Penobscot Indian Louis Neptune, whom Thoreau indicated had been up the mountain "two or three times" by 1846. (10) Neptune's maiden ascent was probably with Jackson. His conduct, however, was that of a model climber, though his experience came from elsewhere, I believe. As they toiled up Katahdin in swirling snow, Neptune took the precaution of fixing their trail with cairns, which, when returning, they were able to follow through the blinding tempest. His foresight may well have saved Jackson's life.

Ironically, if Neptune had not failed to meet Thoreau as arranged, he would have led Thoreau to Katahdin, the consequences of which are too interesting not to speculate about. It seems fair to conclude that with Neptune in charge the party would have followed his former route up Katahdin—that is, over Abol Slide and the Tableland—and that they would have reached the summit. The latter outcome, of course, would have been influenced by the weather, which was uncooperative on September 8. But it was better the day before, and it is then, I speculate, that they would have gone to the top. The scenario might have read: "Arrived at the base of Abol Slide before noon on September 7. Made camp there. Continued up the mountain with Neptune. Reached and explored the summit. Returned before dark." Such a history was lost in a missed appointment.

> *The tops of mountains are among the unfinished parts of the globe, whither it is a slight insult to the gods to climb and pry into their secrets, and try their effect on our humanity. Only daring and insolent men, perchance, go there. Simple races, as savages, do not climb mountains—their tops are sacred and mysterious tracts never visited by them. Pomola is always angry with those who climb to the summit of Ktaadn. (65)*

Neptune's appearance upon Katahdin demolished the myth that Indians did not climb mountains. It is true that as a rule they avoided such eminences, considering them spiritual sanctuaries. The Penobscots believed that Katahdin hosted a triumvirate of spirits—night-wind, storm-bird, and giant Katahdin—whom the white man combined into one being called Pamola. Neptune blamed the snow storm that beset Jackson's expedition on Pamola, who was enraged with their violating his domain. Climbing Katahdin from the West Branch, the Indians told Joseph Chadwick, the surveyor, that they dared not go above treeline lest they not return. Such was the prevalent belief among natives. They could be persuaded to overcome their intimidation, however. On August 13, 1804, Charles Turner Jr., a Massachusetts surveyor, made the first recorded ascent to Katahdin's summit. At Turner's urging, his two Indian companions, allaying their fears, accompanied him to the top.

*The Maine Woods* indicates that its author had not been exposed to either Bailey's or Jackson's published accounts before his trip; he did read both later, however. Knowing their itineraries beforehand would not have altered his plans, I believe.[4] His predilection for the unknown, unmarked, and unusual was too strong.

Thoreau's Katahdin encounter reflected his own style of mountaineering. Whenever possible, he preferred to make his own path, avoiding prescribed passages. Witness, for instance, his ascent two summers earlier of the highest point in Massachusetts, Greylock (3,491 feet), or Saddleback as it was called then. He gained this Berkshire peak by compass, following a straight line to its summit. Later he remembered this tour:

> I at length reached the last house but one, where the path to the summit diverged to the right, while the summit itself rose directly in front. But I determined to follow up the valley to its head, and then find my own route up the steep, as the shorter and more adventurous way. . . . The ascent was by no means difficult or unpleasant, and occupied much less time than it would have taken to follow the path. . . . I have climbed several higher mountains without guide or path, and have found, as might be expected, that it takes only more time and patience commonly than to travel the smoothest highway. It is very rare that you meet with obstacles in this world, which the humblest man has not faculties to surmount.[5]

His descent was also at his own discretion. The method was as important to Thoreau as the results.

## ASCENT

> I have camped out all night on the tops of four mountains,—Wachusett, Saddle-back, Ktaadn, and Monadnock,—and I usually took a ramble over the summit at midnight by moonlight. (June 28, 1852)

Late in the afternoon, from beside Rum Mountain, Thoreau swerved westward from his beeline direction. He did this in order to be near a branch of the Abol for the night. The party's camp, in the ravine to the west of Rum Mountain, was located below treeline—that is, below 3,800 feet. Thoreau was not quite atop Katahdin, but he was higher than he had ever slept before.

From this elevation, Thoreau scaled the mountain twice—neither time by moonlight and neither time to the summit. His first attempt ended on the upper face of the headwall to the west of South Peak. From "a deep and narrow ravine . . . hemmed in by walls of rock," he rose "up the course of the torrent which occupied this" heading for "the nearest, though not the highest peak." (60) He

> . . . *arrived upon a side-hill, or rather side-mountain, where rocks, gray, silent rocks, were the flocks and herds that pastured, chewing a rocky cud at sunset. They looked at me with hard gray eyes, without a bleat or a low. This brought me to the skirt of a cloud, and bounded my walk that night. (61–62)*

From here he returned to his companions.

The next day, September 8, Thoreau tried again. This time he aimed for "the right hand, or highest peak," South Peak, which was "concealed by mist." (62–63) His impression:

> *The mountain seemed a vast aggregation of loose rocks, as if sometime it had rained rocks, and they lay as they fell on the mountain sides, nowhere fairly at rest, but leaning on each other, all rocking-stones, with cavities between, but scarcely any soil or smoother shelf. They were the raw materials of a planet dropped from an unseen quarry, which the vast chemistry of nature would anon work up, or work down, into the smiling and verdant plains and valleys of earth. (63)*

He arrived at "the summit of the ridge" between Baxter and South peaks. His view was obscured—"It was like sitting in a chimney and waiting for the smoke to blow away. It was, in fact, a cloud-factory . . . " His presence, he felt, was unwelcome—"Vast, Titanic,

*Lithograph of Charles Jackson at Katahdin*

AMC Library and Archives

*Mount Katahdin from the West Branch of the Penobscot*

inhuman Nature . . . never made this soil for thy feet, this air for thy breathing." Thoreau suspended his exploration at this point. (63–64)

> *Indeed the summit of a mountain, though it may appear thus regular at a distance, is not, after all, the easiest thing to find, even in clear weather. (July 16, 1858)*

Thoreau was not deceived; he realized that he did not stand on top of Katahdin. On a bright, sunny day, we can imagine his venturing over both South and Baxter peaks, and deciding for himself which one was higher. We wish that this assessment had been made. Even then, however, he might not have been right. No less an alpinist than the Rev. Marcus R. Keep, who climbed Katahdin more than anyone else in this period, established South Peak to be the highest point on the mountain in 1847, as did others in his coterie who had surmounted both summits. Keep held this opinion for the next decade.

*. . . this was primeval, untamed, and forever untamable Nature. . . . Nature was here some-*
*thing savage and awful, though beautiful. . . . Here was no man's garden, but the unhand-*
*selled globe. . . . There was there felt the presence of a force not bound to be kind to man.*
*(69–70)*

Thoreau's reaction to Katahdin was contrary to his expectation. This alpine atmosphere was not the genial climate of Concord and Walden Pond—a far cry from that. This was a hostile, threatening, even repugnant environment. He could not survive here, let alone create. This was his limit to earth's enjoyment. He was not like the seer of the Sierras, John Muir, for whom nature never was too wild, not even when the ground vibrated under his feet.

This encounter, however, did not diminish the saunterer's passion for nature or mountains. His attachment deepened. He continued to explore and to describe New England's peaks. He longed to behold again Maine's highest land, whose memory he cherished forever. Eleven years after his excursion to Katahdin—and after he had missed his last opportunity to return—he revealed to a close friend that the experience was still very much a part of him: "I keep a mountain anchored off eastward a little way, which I ascend in my dreams both awake and asleep."[6]

## RETURN

*Occasionally, as I came down, the wind would blow me a vista open through which I could see*
*the country eastward, boundless forests, and lakes, and streams, gleaming in the sun . . . . (65)*

With no hope for fairer skies, Thoreau descended to meet his companions, none of whom had come to this height. When beneath the clouds, he "could overlook the country west and south for a hundred miles." (66) The course of their return hike lay to the west of their straight-line approach. They stayed with the Abol "continually crossing and recrossing it, leaping from rock to rock, and jumping with the stream down falls of seven or eight feet, or sometimes sliding down on our backs in a thin sheet of water." (67) Then they left the torrent, probably where it turns southward, and, after taking their bearings from the top of a spruce, entered "open land, which went sloping down some miles toward the Penobscot." (69) They reached their bateau at 2 p.m. Two hours later they were on their way home.

Their voyage down the West Branch lasted three days. It can be followed by reversing the itinerary presented in Chapter Nine.

## YOUR ITINERARY

### Baxter State Park

*The kings of England formerly had their forests. . . . Why should not we, who have re-*
*nounced the king's authority, have our national preserves . . . our forests, not to hold the king's*

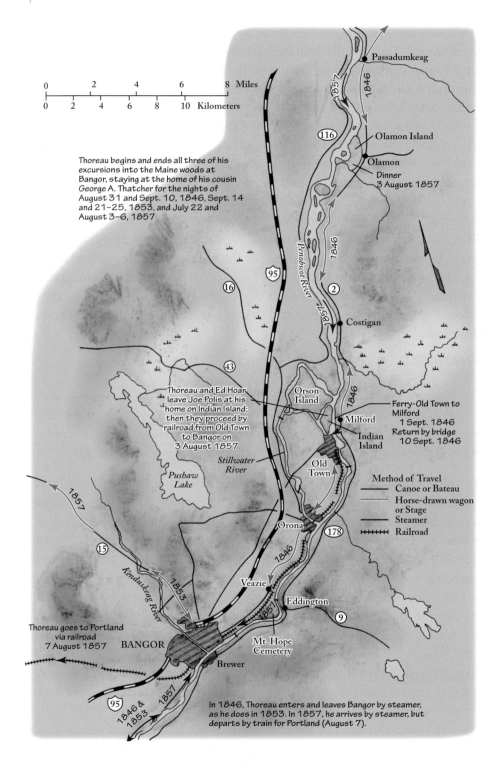

Thoreau begins and ends all three of his excursions into the Maine woods at Bangor, staying at the home of his cousin George A. Thatcher for the nights of August 31 and Sept. 10, 1846, Sept. 14 and 21–25, 1853, and July 22 and August 3–6, 1857

Passadumkeag

Olamon Island

Olamon
Dinner
3 August 1857

116

Penobscot River

95

16

2

43

Costigan

Thoreau and Ed Hoar leave Joe Polis at his home on Indian Island; then they proceed by railroad from Old Town to Bangor on 3 August 1857

Orson Island

Ferry-Old Town to Milford
1 Sept. 1846
Return by bridge
10 Sept. 1846

Milford

Indian Island

Stillwater River

Old Town

Pushaw Lake

Method of Travel
——— Canoe or Bateau
——— Horse-drawn wagon or Stage
——— Steamer
+++++++ Railroad

1857

15

1853

Orona

178

Kenduskeag River

Veazie

Eddington

9

Thoreau goes to Portland via railroad
7 August 1857

BANGOR

Mt. Hope Cemetery

Brewer

95

1846 & 1853

1857

In 1846, Thoreau enters and leaves Bangor by steamer, as he does in 1853. In 1857, he arrives by steamer, but departs by train for Portland (August 7).

Olamon Island, where Thoreau stopped for dinner; (294) and wigwams occupied Mattanawacook Island, opposite Lincoln. Here Louis Neptune lived; Thoreau and Thatcher canoed to the island to make arrangements with him to lead them to Katahdin. (9–10)[4]

The only impediment on this part of the river is the West Enfield Dam. This is portaged on the west (right) side along the road. Instead of an artificial structure, Piscataquis Falls faced nineteenth-century voyagers. Polis navigated the rapids while his crew "walked over the wooden railroad on the eastern shore, about one and a half miles long. . . . . " (292) Minor rips occur below the dam; then the Piscataquis River enters from the west, its course, along with a series of other streams and lakes, providing an old Indian route to Moosehead Lake.[5]

## Old Town

*The Indians on the Island appeared to live quite happily and to be well treated by the inhabitants of Oldtown. (150)*

Approaching Old Town, the river divides, surrounding three large islands. The western channel is called the Stillwater River. If you take the eastern branch, which is recommended, you pass the tip of Orson Island first and then Indian Island, which is still the home of the Penobscot Nation. We pulled ashore on the lawn of St. Ann's Church at the southeast end, which is a pleasant rest stop. A bridge joins this island with a larger one, Marsh, named after its first white settler; on it reside Old Town and the University of Maine (see Additional Places of Interest on page 146).

*Bangor, Maine, in 1835*

Thoreau visited Indian Island on several occasions. On September 22, 1853, he watched a birchbark canoe being made and met a tribal dignitary, Governor John Neptune. When Neptune told Thoreau that at age eighty-nine (actually he was only eighty-six!) he was "going a-moose-hunting that fall, as he had been the previous one," Thoreau remarked: "Probably his companions did the hunting." (147) "This was the first time that I ever called on a governor," the Concordian noted, and it was his last time, too. Neptune was really the lieutenant governor, elected for life in 1816, though he wielded more influence than the governor, John Aitteon, father of Thoreau's 1853 guide, Joseph. The relationship of the two leaders, while never close, deteriorated sharply when the subordinate seduced his superior's spouse. Neptune liked to boast of the many children he had sired, several by Molly Molasses, a Penobscot woman whom Thoreau met in Bangor. (157)

> *His house was a 2-story white one with blinds, the best looking that I noticed there, and as good as an average one on a New England village street. (157–158)*

Thus Thoreau described the home of Joe and Mary Polis, which still stands on Indian Island, just west of the grammar school. Thoreau first met his guide here on July 22, 1857. Twelve days later, at this doorstep, they parted company for the last time, Thoreau then boarding the train at Old Town. As the cars moved south to Bangor, Thoreau no doubt found nostalgic pleasure in recalling his adventures with Joe Polis, treasured memories he never forgot.

The graves of Thoreau's Indian friends are also on this island. In the Old Cemetery, which is the first you come to after crossing the bridge, Joe and Mary Polis and John Neptune are buried. In the New Cemetery, on Center Street opposite the Baptist Church, lies the stone of Joe Aitteon.[6]

## Old Town to Bangor, 13.5 Miles

Before Thoreau's time, "Penobscot" applied to only this part of the river. Signifying "the rocky place" or "at the descending rock," it denoted the rapids, falls, and carries once typical of this segment.[7] Modern dams radically altered the historic countenance of the river. Descending the Penobscot today, you pass Milford Dam, just below Indian Island at Old Town, and the Great Works Dam 1.5 miles farther; the third, Veazie Dam, is three miles above the last, which is at Bangor (see *AMC River Guide: Maine*). This was the only section of the Penobscot that Thoreau did not travel by boat. It is cumbersome to canoe, since the four dams must be portaged, and for a good distance above and below each structure.

On one side, they were hauling the logs up an inclined plane by water-power; on the other, passing out the boards, planks, and sawed timber, and forming them into rafts. The trees were literally drawn and quartered there. (150)

*Penobscot women and children harvesting potatoes on Indian Island in 1900*

After meeting Governor Neptune, Thoreau inspected the Old Town sawmills of General Samuel Veazie (1787–1865). During this era, Veazie acquired all the sawmills between Old Town and Bangor, a total of fifty-two. The General's largest plant, Corporation Mills, was located farther downstream, originally within Bangor's seventh ward. Wanting to avoid the city's tax, the lumber baron asked the legislature to create a new town, Veazie, a request which was granted on March 26, 1853. Its namesake then moved there from Bangor.[8]

The community of Veazie is a riverine town. If it stood any closer to the Penobscot, it would be a floating tenement. You step from your canoe into suburbia. The heart of the hamlet throbs a few blocks west. Veazie Street runs south along the shore to the hydroelectric facility. Residents may think it queer to find their land serving as a portage, but this has been its ancient use. Because the river always has been blocked here—a six-foot falls preceded the dam—and the east bank is too high and steep to negotiate, the flood plain of Veazie has afforded the most advantageous spot from which to enter or leave the river.

Below Veazie Dam is Eddington Bend, where the river turns westward around a bulge of land. The cape, an accumulation of glacial deposits, rises 80 to 100 feet straight out of the water. Its summit, formerly Fort Hill, was an Indian lookout and encampment. In the 1650s the English built a fur trading post here.[9] Thoreau came to Fort Hill twice to search for the remains of the Indian settlement; he found earthenware and arrowheads. (150; August 5, 1857)

Today this elevation is mostly wooded. Second-growth pines, alders, birches, and poplars encroach on paths which lace the area. Houses accommodating Veazie residents sit safely back from the point. Open fields provide photogenic scenes of the valley. The view to the north over the dam is particularly inviting. To the south three giant, black pipes are seen on the horizon. They rise from the Bangor Hydro-Electric substation, where oil, shipped by tanker to Bucksport and by rail from there, burns to produce steam for electricity.

Bangor, Maine, in 1890

Below Eddington Bend, granite monuments stipple a northern hillside. This is Mount Hope Cemetery. Incorporated in 1834, it is Maine's oldest garden cemetery, possibly second in the nation only to Mount Auburn Cemetery (1831) in Cambridge, Massachusetts, after which architect Charles G. Bryant modeled it. This 250-acre sanctuary features a wide variety of trees. Most of the white elms, over 600, have been removed, victims of Dutch elm disease. Smaller Colorado blue spruce have taken their regal place along the entryway. Opposite the superintendent's office are the graves of Thoreau's Bangor hosts, George A. Thatcher and his wife Rebecca Jane Billings, and two of Thoreau's aunts, Jane Thoreau and Maria Thoreau.

## Bangor

*There stands the city of Bangor, fifty miles up the Penobscot, at the head of navigation for vessels of the largest class, the principal lumber depot on this continent, with a population of twelve thousand, like a star on the edge of night, still hewing at the forests of which it is built, already overflowing with the luxuries and refinement of Europe, and sending its vessels to Spain, to England, and to the West Indies for its groceries. . . . (82)*

At midday of July 21, 1857, the steamer from Portland with Thoreau on deck docked at Bangor. The pier lay along the west side of the mouth of a large tributary of the Penobscot, the Kenduskeag, which divides the city. On the opposite shore Indians once lived. They cleared the land under large oaks, farmed the hillside, drew water from a spring, fished the river—*Kenduskeag* means "eel-weir place" in Maliseet—and hunted up the Kenduskeag Valley and at Pushaw Lake, places Thoreau also knew. In the fall of 1853, he botanized along the Kenduskeag, delighting in witch-hazel's yellow bloom. (September 24, 1853) Four years later, he, Thatcher, and Hoar rode six miles north to Pushaw Lake. (August 4, 1857)

Bangor harbor is not the vortex of activity it was when Thoreau was here. Then hundreds of vessels might be tied up loading lumber, while others waited to go out with the tide. Now you have to search for the port: no wharves line the Kenduskeag; no passengers arrive by steamer. You find piers where oil tankers come regularly, even in winter. Though the river always freezes, U.S. Coast Guard ice breakers keep a channel open so that cargo may be delivered to storage facilities, elephantine gray drums along the Penobscot.

After leaving the wharf, Thoreau crossed the Kenduskeag and went to George Thatcher's home at 59 Essex Street. This Greek Revival residence still stands, though it is not open to the public.[10] That evening, Thoreau met Joe Polis at the railroad station, at the corner of Exchange and Washington streets. This depot, along with passenger service to the city, has long since vanished. The Penobscot Plaza is now ensconced here.

Their roles reversed, Thoreau led Polis from the old station to Thatcher's, Polis "puffing under the weight of his canoe." (159) And well might he be breathless, for their course was uphill. They went through Devil's Half Acre, bounded by Washington, Exchange, and Hancock streets, where lumbermen and sailors drank and reveled at taverns and brothels. People I stopped on the street did not know this district by its former name. You might guess this, for its appearance bears little resemblance to its nineteenth-century identity. Today, you pass spacious parking lots, tall bank buildings, car dealers, churches, food stores, and residences—as you retrace the first portage Polis and Thoreau ever made. This was a far cry from the Mud Pond Carry!

The following morning, the stage called for the rusticators at Thatcher's. The Bangor House (1834), across town on the southeast corner of Main and Union, was the next stop. This hotel, already famous for its hospitality, cuisine, and distinguished guests, Senator Daniel Webster among them, was designed by Bangor's leading architect, Charles G. Bryant, who chose to copy Boston's Tremont House (1829), America's first luxury hotel. Though the latter is gone, the Bangor house is alive and well.

Renovations, in fact, helped restore it closer to the original. The interior, however, has been altered to accommodate its new senior and handicapped residents, who since 1979 have occupied this historic landmark.

> *At Bangor House, four men boarded the stage. Their leader was a handsome man about thirty years old, of good height, but not apparently robust, of gentlemanly dress and faultless toilet. . . . He had a fair white complexion, as if he had always lived in the shade, and an intellectual face, and with his quiet manners might have passed for a divinity student who had seen something of the world. (161)*

As they rode to Greenville, Thoreau became acquainted with this passenger. His name was Hiram L. Leonard, his reputation, as "the chief white hunter of Maine." (161) He not only used guns, but made them as well. However, it was not guns, but split-bamboo fly rods, which Leonard began producing at his Bangor gun shop in 1871, that spread his fame far beyond New England. What Thoreau did not learn is that he and the "great white hunter" shared a common enthusiasm: playing their flutes in the wilderness.[11]

## BANGOR TO SANDY POINT, 25 MILES

*A withdrawn, wooded, and somewhat mountainous country. (August 6, 1857)*

Old mariners called this part of the Penobscot the "Bangor River." Tides control the river's direction of flow and depth to Bangor. Fresh water yields to salt below Marsh Bay. Islands dissolve except for the venerable Verona, which almost plugs the river's mouth. Shores are narrow and wide, muddy and rocky, pastoral and populated. Towns like Winterport make you feel like staying. Low hills scallop the landscape. Thoreau steamed up and down the Bangor River several times, and rode along both shores, to Belfast (May 11, 1838) and to Bucksport (August 6, 1857).

# Penobscot Bay

*Next I remembered that the Camden Hills attracted my eyes, and afterward the hills about Frankfort. (85)*

Beyond Sandy Point, the river enters the magnificent Penobscot Bay, largest on Maine's coast. This expanse offers a splendid voyage. Thoreau steamed its length, and sailed its width from Belfast to Castine. (May 13–14, 1838) Countless coves, harbors, and islands beckon to be explored. One special place is Camden. Anchor in its lovely harbor, stay at the Whitehall Inn, or camp at Camden Hills State Park. Rise early in the morning and climb Mt. Battie (800 feet). Behold the sleeping sailboats beneath you, and Thoreau's passageway across the speckled sea.

---

## Additional Places of Interest

### Orono

#### *University of Maine*

The resources of this institution are many and diverse, natural and artificial. Exploration of the Fay Hyland Botanical Plantation along the Stillwater River is rewarded by more than 300 species of trees and shrubs, plus various herbs, ferns, and clubmosses. The Dwight D. Demeritt Forest and University Farms offer enjoyable walks. The Raymond H. Fogler Library contains a wealth of knowledge about Maine; especially valuable are the manuscripts of Fannie Hardy Eckstorm and her father, Manly Hardy.

## Brewer

### *Fannie Hardy Eckstorm House*

From Bangor a pleasant stroll across the Penobscot River on Chamberlain Bridge brings you into the city of Brewer, the birthplace of Fannie Hardy Eckstorm (1865–1946). After crossing the bridge, proceed eastward on Wilson Street to number 159. This two-story dwelling was Manly and Emeline Hardy's home, where their children, including Fannie, were raised. It later became the home of Charlotte Hardy, Fannie's sister. Continue on to the private residence at 173 Wilson Street. Here Fannie Hardy Eckstorm lived from 1899 until her death; this is where she wrote her most famous works on the Penobscot Valley.

## Maine Woods Landforms

### *Eskers*

*There were singular long ridges hereabouts, called "horsebacks," covered with ferns. (284)*

Thoreau made this observation at Grindstone Falls on the west side of the Penobscot's East Branch. His perception was correct. This landform—known locally as a horseback or whaleback ridge, or generally as an *esker* (Irish: ridge of mountains) or *os* (Swedish: ridge)—parallels the lower East Branch. Thoreau no doubt recognized this esker from his intimacy with them in Concord, though he also learned about them from his reading of Charles Jackson's report. Jackson climbed this East Branch embankment, nowhere more than seventy feet above the surrounding plain, and viewed Katahdin from its crest.[12]

This esker was more fully explored by geologist George H. Stone, who canoed the East Branch in 1879. Stone described its composition of "clay overlain by sand and gravel, all very nearly horizontally stratified," and its ridge shape of "steep lateral slopes on both east and west sides . . . usually densely covered by vegetation. . . . " Stone also determined that "Thoreau's esker," as he referred to it, belonged to a larger network, which he named Katahdin after the source of the glacial river that deposited the material forming it. He delineated its expanse thusly: running south along the East Branch for fourteen miles, fording the Penobscot River at Medway, trending southward, re-crossing the Penobscot at South Lincoln, and continuing south through Greenfield to Columbia near the sea—a length of 125 miles, he estimated.[13] The section between South Lincoln and Greenfield is now called the Enfield Horseback. On September 1, 1846, Thoreau traveled over this esker by carriage on his way to Enfield. *The Maine Woods*, however, is silent about its presence. (8)

The esker of the Penobscot Valley is one of the best examples of its kind anywhere in the world. From the air, where its configuration is most conspicuous, it resembles a giant molehill gently winding down the map, its maker in search of sustenance. A force greater than the mole's, however, is responsible for its creation. It is the *oeuvre* of the Laurentide Ice Sheet that

10,000 years ago buried New England under a frozen mass several thousand feet thick. When the great thaw occurred, rivers of meltwater flowed through the glacier, carrying sediments which were laid down on the landscape in the form of long, narrow, sinuous spines. On these elevated arteries, animals and Indians walked, trails developed, and roads were built.

Eskers are another of Maine's natural laureates. They are nowhere in the United States more abundant and attractive, yet they are an endangered species. So valuable is their contents that many have been disfigured. They are excavated for sand and gravel which is used in road construction. Almost half of the eskers near Bangor, for example, have been spoiled. Like plants and animals, landforms have a right to live and deserve our respect. These remarkable features of our ancient heritage should be preserved.

## AFTERWORD

Thoreau's "wildest country" was a site of travel and meditation long before I visited it to retrace his steps. In fact, there was a flurry of activity in the region in the mid-nineteenth century. The literary-artistic exploration of the Maine woods had its roots in this period, when the travels of two of its most evocative interpreters, Thoreau and the artist Frederic Edwin Church, coincided. Both explored and chronicled this place of Maine's highest ground, largest lake, and grandest boreal forest. Of the two, Church lived the longer life and spent far more time in Maine. Each left, in his own way, indelible images.

In this afterword, I will share some thoughts on how Thoreau's trips interacted with and even motivated those of others, especially Church. I will also examine how Thoreau and Church influenced some other writers and artists who came to the North Country, at least in part, due to them.

### The 1850s

It was August 1856. Ten years after climbing Katahdin, Thoreau was at home in Concord, Massachusetts., though he would leave for an eight-day trip to Vermont and New Hampshire on September fifth. Meanwhile, under a cloudless sky on Maine's Moosehead Lake, two Connecticut natives—now New Yorkers—talked deck-side: thirty-year-old painter Frederic Edwin Church and Theodore Winthrop, the future author, who would be twenty-eight in September. They had boarded a steamboat in Greenville that morning, stopped mid-lake to dine at Kineo House with "lumbermen and moose-hunters," Winthrop said, before continuing northward. Suddenly in the east appeared their destination, Mount Katahdin. Their conversation turned to mountains.

The year before, in August 1855, Church and Winthrop had been on Mount Desert on the Maine Coast. They were part of a large party organized by Charles Tracy, a New York attorney who taught Winthrop enough law in a year to be admitted to the bar that summer. On the 8th, Church climbed Newport Mountain (now Champlain, 1,058 feet). Winthrop arrived later that day and had plenty of pleasant rambles about the green granite isle before leaving at the end of the month. Church had come here for the first time five years earlier. At that time he spent six weeks exploring, ascending the island's highest peak, Cadillac (1,532 feet), and making sketches, one of which resulted in the painting *Fog off Mount Desert* (1850). That same summer of 1850, Winthrop made a walking tour of the Alps, without any "great ascensions," his sister wrote. South of Mont Blanc, he climbed Cramont (8,000 feet, he noted) from the Italian village of Courmayeur (4,028 feet).

Church was encouraged to see Maine for himself by the Hudson River School painter Thomas Cole, who had come to Mount Desert in the summer of 1844—just after meeting Church in Hartford, Connecticut, and agreeing to take him on as a pupil. Another incentive for Church's Down East presence, according to art historian John Wilmerding, was Thoreau's "Ktaadn," which was published in five installments of the *Union Magazine of Literature and Art*, starting in July 1848. Extracts also appeared in Horace Greeley's *New York Tribune* of November 17 and 18, 1848.

Surely, Church told Winthrop of his prior visit to Moosehead, in the summer of 1852, when he had stopped at Mount Kineo long enough to sketch its features. Then he traveled via the West and East branches of the Penobscot River (most likely) to Hunt's Farm, hiking west to Katahdin Lake. From there, Church drew Katahdin and, as Winthrop later related, "scuffled up its eastern land-slides with a squad of lumbermen." Church's three-foot-high, four-and-a-half foot-long marvel *Mount Ktaadn* resulted from this journey; he exhibited it on April 19, 1853, at the National Academy of Design.

Eleven days before his *Mount Ktaadn* exhibit opened, Church left New York for a six-month trip to South America. In Colombia and Ecuador, the northernmost reaches of the magnificent Andes inspired him. In September, while Thoreau was seeing Moosehead Lake, the West Branch, and Chesuncook Lake for the first time, Church was ascending the volcano Chimborazo (20,577 feet) to snowline. This peak was featured in his famous *The Heart of the Andes* (1859), exhibited first in New York on April 27, 1859, and described by Winthrop in an essay published in *Harper's Weekly* in April 1861.

That same summer of 1853, Winthrop explored the Pacific Northwest, and reveled in seeing mountains everywhere. The grandest, Rainier (14,410 feet), whose native name Tacoma (big peak) he much preferred, he first saw from his canoe on Puget Sound in August—"a giant mountain dome of snow." Then he passed it on horseback and crossed the Naches Pass (4,800 feet) with Indian guides to the Dalles on the Columbia River. From there, on the first of September, Winthrop "mounted a fresh horse, and went galloping along on my way across the continent." A Rainier glacier now bears Winthrop's name.

While Winthrop communed with Rainier, on Saturday, August 13, 1853, the poet James Russell Lowell took passage on the steamer *Moosehead* from Greenville. He arrived there late the previous night after an eighteen-hour coach and mud-wagon ride from Waterville, Maine, which he had reached by train from his Cambridge, Massachusetts, home the day before. Except for a few clearings on the shore, the lake appeared to Lowell "wholly primeval." At Kineo, Lowell found only the tavern owned by Squire Barrows. There he spent two days before paddling with guides and hunters to the Northwest Carry, portaging over to Seboomook Lake, and descending the West Branch in search of moose into the cold early morning. After a two-and-a-half-hour sleep, he and his traveling companions "started at half past four" back to Kineo, arriving in time for dinner—in the 19th century, this meal was eaten in the middle of the day—and an ascent of Mount Kineo, whose shape reminded Lowell of the island of Capri.

On August 9, 1854, Thoreau noted in his journal that *Walden* was published. Shortly thereafter, Thomas Wentworth Higginson, the pastor of the Free Church of Worcester,

Massachusetts, wrote to thank Thoreau for *Walden*. The publisher James Fields of Ticknor and Fields of Boston had sent him an advance copy. Higginson also bought two copies for one dollar each, one for himself and one for an aspiring young writer named Harriet Prescott. On June 29, 2005, Higginson's inscribed copy of *Walden* sold at Christie's auction house for $216,000.

In early September 1855, inspired by Thoreau's excursion to Katahdin, Higginson left for Maine with five women and five men. They traveled by train from Boston to Portland, then took an overnight steamer to Bangor. After that leg of the trip, they rode on an open wagon northward along the Penobscot River to Greenbush, where they spent the second night, and spent the third night at the South Moluncas Hotel. The following noon, an eighteen-mile ride found them, as Higginson wrote, "beyond towns with names," eating dinner in a sixteen-year-old tavern in a small settlement called township number 3. Hunt's, where they expected to spend that night, "was only ten miles, by the road, if it only had been a road," Higginson related. "But the ride turned out to be a walk, for most of us, and the first five miles took nearly three hours. And the lumber road made Pinkham Notch look smooth, and the North Conway paths appear English lawns."

Instead of Hunt's, they reached the farmhouse of John Stacy, who fortuitously joined them as a guide. Stacy had helped the Reverend Marcus Keep cut the first path to Katahdin, which the group would soon follow. During dinner at Hunt's the next day, hearing that Frederic Church had just been there, Higginson and his coterie wished the artist had stayed long enough "to accompany and illustrate our march." After the meal, they crossed the East Branch and walked six "leisurely miles." He said this trip was "too delicious to be real, and too genuine to be ideal," stopping at sunset at a camp made ready by the guides who had preceded them. Away at seven the next morning, they walked seven miles, crossing Wassataquoik Stream, coming to Katahdin Lake at two o'clock, where "trout and tranquility ruled the hour." "It was the most personal mountain" Higginson had ever seen, more so than any of the White Mountains or Monadnock.

The next morning they "walked four miles to Roaring Brook," then after dinner "began to go up in earnest" three more miles to Avalanche Brook. The final two miles "passed without knowing it" before camping in the woods by the brook. The next morning broke cold and clear—"such a day as one dreams of for the great days of history"—and they climbed up a great slide to the top in three hours. After walking another mile in an hour, they felt satisfied and turned around. Back at their camp, much merriment blessed their meal of partridge with fresh mountain cranberry sauce. A ten-mile hike the next day brought them to Katahdin Lake again. Higginson wrote that they "loved it all the more, because we had a foreboding that it would be our last night in the woods; and so it proved." Warm as the next day was, they made the thirteen difficult miles back to Hunt's in a determined, brisk "style that delighted" John Stacy.

Eleven months later, Church and Winthrop had their discussion of mountains on Moosehead Lake. Their steamer, which had picked them up from Greenville, left them at the Northeast Carry, which they crossed by "ox-locomotive." In this system, one great ox pulled over a wooden railroad one great go-cart loaded with their gear. "A birch canoe is the right thing in the right place," Winthrop believed, as they descended the West Branch, their craft steered by its owner, their Indian guide, Cancut. "Sun-cooked Chesuncook we traversed by aid of our blanket-sail," Winthrop happily reported. "Katahdin lost nothing by approach," they found, "as it grew bigger it grew better." Continuing down the West Branch, walking the three-mile Ripogenus Carry, they camped opposite Abol Stream, with Katahdin in clear view. From here, with Cancut's guidance, they climbed Katahdin. Despite fog, mist, and chill, some vistas opened: on the southern horizon they saw "the heights of Mount Desert." They tramped about, ate their fill of blueberries and cranberries, and "long after noon" descended, reaching their camp. "In the last hour of light" they broke camp and headed downstream.

In 1857, the year Thoreau made his longest and last Maine woods journey, the *Atlantic Monthly* was established with James Russell Lowell as editor. Lowell, through Emerson, asked for a Thoreau essay on his 1857 Maine excursion. Though Thoreau lectured on that trip in Concord on February 25, 1858, to protect the privacy of his guide Joe Polis, he instead submitted "Chesuncook," which Lowell published in installments in the June, July, and August issues. This essay was Thoreau's account of his 1853 excursion and was included in *The Maine Woods*. Lowell's omission of a crucial sentence—the one that proclaimed the pine tree as "immortal as I am, and perchance will go to as high a heaven, there to tower above me still"—upset Thoreau and caused a rift between the two. Resigning from the *Atlantic* in May 1861, Lowell lived thirty more years, to August 1891, distinguishing himself in letters and as ambassador to the Court of St. James in the United Kingdom.

### The 1860s

The 1860s brought the deaths of Theodore Winthrop and Henry Thoreau, but the gifts of posthumous publication of their writings. The *Atlantic*, now under James T. Fields, serialized from August to December 1862 (excluding October), "Life in the Open Air," Winthrop's account of his August 1856 travels in Maine with Church. It was published in a book of the same title in May 1863, along with his "The Heart of the Andes." Neither Winthrop, who was shot in the Civil War on June 10, 1861, nor Thoreau, who died at home on May 6, 1862, lived to see this in print. In November 1862 Winthrop's memoir *The Canoe and the Saddle* appeared, which, along with his novels *Cecil Dreeme* and *John Brent*, greatly enlarged his audience. *The Maine Woods* was published on May 28, 1864. Higginson reviewed it for the September issue of the *Atlantic*. Higginson's long, outstanding life in letters—it included the mentoring of Helen Hunt Jackson and Emily Dickinson, among others—lasted until May 9, 1911, when he died at age eighty-seven. Church married Isabel Carnes on June 14, 1860, had children (one named for Winthrop), and built an elaborate Persian-style home on the Hudson River, called Olana, now a museum open to the public. Yet he continued to travel in Maine. He became, in critic John K. Howat's words, the "chief artistic discoverer and canonizer of Maine's coasts and woodlands."

### Late 1870s

On Sunday, September 8, 1877, at noon, Church arrived at Katahdin Lake from Boston. The trip—which required a train trip, a wagon ride, and a thirteen-mile hike—took almost four days. He traveled with ten men: three other artists (Sanford Robinson Gifford, Lockwood de Forest III, and Horace W. Robbins), two "professional men" (M. La Rose and A. L. Holley), and five guides. They walked about the lake, finding "two fine, sandy beaches" at its head, fished for trout (a sport at which Gifford excelled), sketched, and greatly relished their evening meals, campfires, pipes, punch, stories, and "sweet, healthful sleep." Holley and Church ascended "a slide in the north lobe of the Great Basin" to the Tableland, from which Church went to explore North Basin, while others attained the summit. Though Gifford, de Forest, and Robbins departed on the 21st, Church and Holley remained four more days, Church working assiduously in a variety of weathers. "One bright morning, the whole crest of Ktaadn was covered with snow, and also a part of the interior of the Great Basin," Holley wrote.

Afterward Holley, under the pseudonym of Arbor Ilex, recounted their sojourn for *Scribner's Monthly* of May 1878. His narrative, while original, bears resonances of both Thoreau and Winthrop—particularly in his descriptions of camp, gear, food, daily routine, and expenses. One wonders how much they were a presence, a part of the conversation on this journey. Holley's pronouncement—"Few views of mountains in any country exceed that from the southern shore of Lake Ktaadn, in combined grandeur and beauty"—revealed at least one reason for the strong appeal of this place. Holley was equally enthralled with the view from the top of Katahdin: "the most remarkable and the most beautiful I have ever seen." Ten illustrations in woodcut form accompanied the text: five by Church; three by Robbins; and one by Gifford—*Crest of Ktaadn*—and one by de Forest—*Ktaadn from Creek at West End of Lake*. The headpiece is Church's *Ktaadn, from the South Shore of the Lake*, shown in a studio displayed on a giant easel, with attached palette, a walking stick leaning against the canvas, and an open paint box on the rug beneath.

In late August 1879, another artist, Thomas Sedgwick Steele of Hartford, Connecticut, with a "photographic artist," an insurance executive, and three guides descended the East Branch to Hunt's farm. A diminutive pen-and-ink drawing in Steele's *Canoe and Camera* (p. 130) shows their big, white canvas tent on the shore upriver from Hunt's log house and barn, with open fields extending up the hill behind it. Here they learned that a birch-bark canoe, "twenty-eight feet long, over four feet wide (midships)," was being made for Frederic Church, who had "recently purchased four hundred acres of land on Milinockett [sic] Lake," and that men from Hunt's were going there to "erect three substantial log camps."

Historian Fannie Hardy Eckstorm thought it was unlikely that Church's bark canoe was as large as Steele described, and I would concur.

Katahdin Lake was not on Steele's itinerary, though it could be reached from Hunt's, he wrote, "with little difficulty" on horseback to within two miles of its peak. Instead, scrambling up Mount Hunt (1,525 feet, on the west side of the river) in two hours on Sunday morning, August 24, he saw Katahdin, emerging from storm clouds drenched in rainbow colors. He wanted only to "be left alone for hours, to watch the changes of the landscape and hear the secret voice and dread revelations of these magnificent mountains."

Two days after Steele's ascent of Mount Hunt, a college student named Theodore Roosevelt passed through Hunt's with woodsman William Sewall of Island Falls and others. Roosevelt likely knew of Church's 1877 adventure from the article by Holley in *Scribner's*. Like Church, the future president of the United States proceeded afoot up Wassataquoik Stream, reaching the head of Katahdin Lake the next day, where he camped. On the 29th, Roosevelt ascended Katahdin, most likely via the Great Basin, returning for the night to his Katahdin Lake camp. Then he returned to Harvard in late September for his senior year and celebrated his twenty-first birthday in late October.

Church was indeed at his camp at Millinocket Lake in August 1879. Evidently his lodgings were being built then, most likely by the crew from Hunt's. In September, Church and his wife welcomed the artists Sanford Robinson Gifford and Jervis McEntee with their wives. Beset by inclement weather—"rain which fell half the time, and wind which blew nearly all the other half," Gifford exaggerated—they did more fishing than sketching. Nonetheless, Gifford's oil painting *Mount Katahdin from Lake Millinocket* was ready for sale by the following May. It showed Katahdin under cloudless sky with snow on its crest and down its south side, shore and islands burnt, and calm water rumpled enough to blur the reflections of mountain and passengers in two birch-bark canoes coming from the right (east) side. The next summer, Gifford sojourned at Lake Superior for his health without benefit; he died in New York on August 29, 1880, at age fifty-eight.

## INSPIRATION

Since the time of Thoreau and Church, many others have followed in their footsteps. I have selected a handful of other writers and artists whose travels were influenced by Thoreau and Church to profile briefly here.

### John Burroughs (1837–1921)

At the time of Gifford's death in late August 1880, the famed literary naturalist John Burroughs, of the Catskill Mountains and the Hudson River, made his way up the Kennebec River valley into the interior of Maine. He knew Thoreau's writings intimately, quoting and critiquing them. They shared a penchant for staying put and exploring the near-at-hand. Burroughs and his guide camped first at Pleasant Pond, before walking seven miles through the woods to the seven-mile-long Moxie Pond. Settled "amid the birches, poplars, and white cedars near the head of the lake," according to Burroughs, they swam, fished, and shot mergansers and a loon, which Burroughs kept stuffed at home. They climbed Bald Mountain (2,630 feet), now on the Appalachian Trail. "[T]he most impressive mountain-top I had ever seen," Burroughs wrote in his essay, "A Taste of Maine Birch," from which "in a clearer atmosphere the foot of Moosehead Lake would have been visible," only sixteen miles to the northeast. He related that the "highest and most striking mountain to be seen was Mount Bigelow, rising above Dead River, far to the west."

In June 1883, Burroughs made a literary pilgrimage to Concord with Richard Watson Gilder, the editor of the *Century* magazine, to which Burroughs was a contributor. On the 28th, they walked to Walden Pond and talked with Edward Emerson, whose father, Ralph Waldo, had died the previous year, in April 1882. Though Concord impressed Burroughs—he wrote of "its amplitude, its mellowness, its homelike air, its great trees, its broad avenues, its good houses"—the village revealed to him little of Thoreau, noting "I saw nothing in Concord that recalled Thoreau."

### John Muir (1838–1914)

Ten years later, on June 8, 1893, the president of the newly formed Sierra Club of San Francisco, John Muir, and the associate editor of the *Century*, Robert Underwood Johnson, did likewise: They sauntered to Walden in the afternoon and dined with Edward Emerson that evening. Unlike Burroughs, however, they found Thoreau everywhere, visiting Thoreau's grave, his residence, and his friend, John Shepard Keyes. A week earlier in New York, Johnson had introduced Muir and Burroughs; that was their first meeting, although their essays had appeared together in *Scribner's Monthly* of November 1878.

In October 1894, the Century Company published Muir's first book, *The Mountains of California*. On June 22, 1896, Burroughs and Muir met again. This time Muir came up the Hudson River to Burroughs's writing cabin, Slabsides, in West Park, New York.

On October 21, 1898, at 11 a.m., a slender man of sixty stepped off the Bangor train at Greenville. Muir was making a solo train transit of the Northern Forest, through the Adirondack, Green, White, and Longfellow mountains. After waiting two-and-a-half hours in Greenville, Muir rode the Canadian Pacific along eleven miles of Moosehead Lake's west shore before the cars turned west to pass along the south end of Brassua Lake and Long Pond, and went into Quebec. This gave Muir an opportunity to savor the wilderness he had read about in *The Maine Woods*, twenty-eight years earlier, during the first spring of his Yosemite Valley residency. In this brief Maine visit, Muir absorbed the lake's "picturesque islands," surrounding hills and trees—maple, birch, ash, tamarac, spruce, pine. Clouds obscured Katahdin; possibly Kineo, too (Muir's journal and letter home are silent about them). Nor did he draw any of his wonderful sketches of the landscape, which occupy his journal in other places. Unlike Church and Thoreau, Muir had not come to Maine to make art. Had he had the time to paddle Moosehead with Indian guides, as he had in Alaska's Glacier Bay, and to climb Katahdin, as he had so many Sierra Nevada peaks, he might have inscribed this place in literature. An avid reader, Muir cherished above all the direct contact with nature. As he wrote of mountains to Emerson, "One day[']s exposure will do more than cartloads of books."

### Herbert Wendell Gleason (1855–1937)

The year after Muir's Maine visit, Herbert Wendell Gleason, who had been a Congregational pastor and editor in Minneapolis, returned with his wife to their native Massachusetts, to pursue his true calling: landscape photography and illustrated travel lectures. He was forty-four, and would pursue this artistic vocation for the rest of his life.

In the fall of 1899, Gleason began taking pictures of Thoreau's world. During the late summer and early fall of 1900, he roamed about Moosehead Lake with his camera. Two extraordinary pictures show his characterization of this place. The first—taken on September 22 from atop Squaw Mountain on the southwest end of Moosehead Lake— looked eastward. Squaw Pond, a white circle fringed with trees, illuminated the high, dark forest on the lower half of the frame. Below, more light filled the southern part of Mountain View Pond and Moosehead Lake, the north end of Moose Island, even tiny Black Sand Island off its north end, and Burnt Jacket Mountain on the lake's east side. Distant clouds, a line of cumulus, culminated in one large cauliflower over the Lily Bay Mountain.

A week later Gleason looked down from Mount Kineo, at mid-lake, and made another image. In the photograph, below him extends southward the black ground of the Kineo peninsula, with its various white buildings, connecting paths, and roads, though not a person in sight. Surrounding this hotel complex is a vast white space of perfectly open, still water. Sandbar Island holds prominence in the distant center. Fingers of black lowland reach out to one another. Beyond is a slim bit of sky above the hills. Even with the close focus on the Kineo resort, the lake's presence predominates. In the absence of humanity— not even a boat, just pure spaciousness—Gleason reveals the lake's beauty as superior to Kineo's. Even with human activity, nature still prevails here.

In the summer of 1907 while Gleason visited Muir at his home in Martinez, California, Muir learned that Gleason's art in photogravure graced *The Writings of Henry D. Thoreau*, Walden Edition, published in twenty volumes in 1906 by Boston publisher Houghton Mifflin. Muir sent an order for the set back to Boston with Gleason. In the third volume, *The Maine Woods*, Muir saw Gleason's portrait of Moosehead Lake from Mount Kineo. After Muir's death, Houghton Mifflin published *The Writings of John Muir*. The ten-volume Manuscript Edition (1916–1924) and the eight-volume Sierra Edition (1917–1918) both contained Gleason's and others' illustrations.

### Marsden Hartley (1877–1943)

In January 1877—the same year of Church's sojourn at Katahdin Lake—Marsden Hartley was born in Lewiston, Maine. Sixty-two years later, in October 1939, Hartley, like Church, painted Katahdin from Katahdin Lake, though he did not climb the mountain. Guided by the district's head game warden, Caleb Scribner of Patten, the two men drove—the car had replaced the carriage—to Avalanche Field. No longer the arduous trek from Hunt's on the East Branch that Church and others had endured, the four-mile walk east from Avalanche Field (1,196 feet) through woods, rain, mud, and darkness to the lake (1,022 feet) was challenging enough for Hartley, however. Hartley and Scribner stayed at the camp of Oliver and Della Cobb on the lake's southern shore. The Cobbs put Hartley in the last log cabin on the right, which he sketched in pencil; another cabin held his art supplies. According to Della Cobb, Hartley sat on the long dock, working, making "every moment count." He "painted vigorously" in all kinds of weather, even the first alpine snow of the season, which came near the end of his eight-day stay.[1]

Back at his Bangor home, Hartley felt revived. Katahdin Lake was heaven. There he had for sure "seen God." He plunged into painting the mountain—some eighteen versions, Scott says—and into the reading of the many volumes of Thoreau's *Journal* at the Bangor Public Library. "Henry has immortalized himself in relation to the mountain for all time," he wrote. Hartley felt a strong connection to Thoreau. These twin passions—Katahdin and Thoreau—lasted to his death four years later, on September 2, 1943.

### Richard E. Winslow III (1934–)

Boston-born historian Richard Winslow, who has lived in Portsmouth, New Hampshire, since 1983, began his canoeing of Maine's lakes and rivers in 1963. For two summers, he and David Faxon, as counselors at Dr. Johnson's Camps (now Camp Laurel South) on Crescent Lake, east of Casco, led campers through many bodies of water. They included Panther Pond, Sebago Lake, the Belgrade Lakes, the Dead River, Flagstaff Lake, Long Lake, Kezar Lake, the Saco River, Cupsuptic, Mooselookmeguntic, and the Richardson lakes.

A decade later, on June 27, 1974, Winslow was a counselor again and put into the Penobscot West Branch with Wes Herrick and youths from Herrick's Camp Wanderlust (which no longer exists) on Molunkus Lake. It was Winslow's first Allagash trip; it was Herrick's forty-fourth, having made his first in 1930, at age twenty. A month later they completed their journey at Michaud Farm. (Two days later, July 29, in Greenville, I started my travels in Thoreau's Maine woods.)

In July 1989, Winslow made his first trip—the Moose River Loop—with the Conovers, Garrett and Alexandra, professional guides with North Woods Ways in Willimantic, Maine. He continued to travel with them. In early October 1993, they spent five days on the Allagash River. The next summer, at Allagash Lake they agreed that it was "the most beautiful lake in Maine." In 1996, they canoed the West Branch and Chesuncook Lake, a trip they repeated twice at five-year intervals; in autumn 2006 they were guests at the Chesuncook Lake House.

In March 2007, Winslow, at seventy-two, reflected on his many canoe trips in Maine and elsewhere—his longest covered more than a thousand miles of the Canadian Arctic with seventeen others in two summer months of 1988—and affirmed, "I have thoroughly enjoyed every trip for the last forty-four years." And he has plans for more canoeing, writing, and swimming in the Atlantic Ocean at New Castle Beach, a short walk from his home.

### Tony Foster (1946–)

On August 17, 1984, Tony Foster and I paddled up Moosehead Lake. Connie Judkins of Folsom's Air Service in Greenville explained that we would encounter "prevailing westerlies for a few days." The westerlies thrived, died, and revived. Waves broke over the bow of our Old Town ABS canoe. Water sloshed about our packs. The rough going kept us to the lee of islands whenever possible. Thoreau had brought us together. Foster had come from Cornwall, England, to paint Thoreau's New England, the first watercolorist to do so seriously.

After a cold start from windy Moose Island, where Foster did some painting before breakfast, an exquisite day unfolded. We reached Sand Bar Island in early afternoon. The island's owner and patron saint, Lee Salk, whom I first met there on August 18, 1980, welcomed us and extended every kindness. After lunch, Foster worked all afternoon on a painting of Kineo. Finishing a delicious supper with honeydew melons and lemon, and looking forward to sleeping in a guest cottage, Foster smacked his lips. "Now this is what I call camping."

Early the next morning, the wind came from the south. Fog rose off the lake. Only bits of sun penetrated a sky closed so completely. From the island's dock, Tony painted the view east looking toward Lily Bay Mountain. After Lee Salk's breakfast of blueberry pancakes, Foster wanted to take him with us.

We reached Kineo in calm waters at three o'clock, in an hour and forty minutes. Foster painted from an elevated lookout on Mount Kineo for a couple of hours.

The next day we paddled to Northeast Carry. As we were trying to decide how to portage our gear, the proprietor of the Northeast Carry Inn, W. J. LaCrosse, asked, "Haul you across?" "How much?" we asked. "Ten dollars." Not wanting to violate the spirit of our trip, we deliberated, and then compromised. We walked over with our canoe and one pack; he put two more packs, life preservers, paddles, pad, painting board, and tube for paper into his 1942 Dodge truck, and drove over for the same price.

The rest of our canoe journey has been related elsewhere (see Further Readings). After returning from Telos Lake, we climbed Katahdin on August 30. Foster carried all his painting gear in anticipation of the scenery, only to be befogged above tree line. Nonetheless, Foster made art of the moment by using photographs of the sign at Thoreau Spring and of himself barely visible in the fog at the summit to put with two small paintings to make a collage called *Katahdin Summit*. The next day he painted Katahdin from Upper Togue Pond. On September 1, we returned to Moosehead Lake. The passage from Rockwood to Kineo was too rough, so we camped at Woody's on the Moose River. The next morning we crossed to Kineo, climbed the mountain, and Foster worked on the scene for six hours. We paddled back to Rockwood in twenty minutes, a stiff north wind beating at our side, both kneeling for balance, waves spilling into Foster's lap. We were greatly relieved to be ashore.

Spring 1985 saw the opening of Tony Foster's exhibit of "Thoreau's Country: A Visual Diary," at the Yale Center for British Art in New Haven, Conn. Here was *Four Days on Moosehead Lake*, which showed a view of southern Moosehead from Mount Kineo. Unlike Gleason, however, Foster omitted the Kineo resort, choosing instead to foreground the blue lake's white-streaked surface, almost surf-like in places. Peninsulas, islands—Sand Bar is distinct in the center—their green trees bleached by the bright sun. Beyond, the mountains—looking barren in mauve and deeper purple—divide lake and sky. Your eyes rise upward here, as Foster placed his majestic, white clouded sky above the water, land, and viewer.

Since returning from New England, Foster has painted a variety of landscapes all over the world, including John Muir's Sierra Nevada, the Grand Canyon, and the volcanic peaks of the Pacific Northwest—Rainier, Baker, Adams. He has also put to paper those in Montserrat, Bolivia, and Hawaii, as well as Greenland's icebergs and glaciers. On a 225.8-mile, sixteen-day raft trip on the Colorado River, he made a painting a day. These works are now collected at the Denver Art Museum. He seems to leave out no piece of geography. In 1994 he was elected to the Royal Geographical Society. He still pursues his creative journeys, captured in various catalogues and his retrospective book, with delight.

### Evelyn Dunphy (1940–)

During spring 2007, Maine schoolchildren studied Church's painting, *Mount Katahdin from Millinocket Camp* (1853). One day an artist appeared at the Woodside Elementary School in Topsham, dressed and equipped for work in the wild. Evelyn Dunphy told the attentive fourth graders what it was like to do what Church had done, and compared his time in Maine to hers. A decade earlier, in October 1997, she had driven from her home on the mid-Maine coast to Baxter State Park and parked at Avalanche Field. She walked three and a half miles east to Katahdin Lake, camped, and painted the mountain for her first time, as Marsden Hartley had done almost sixty years earlier—and Church as early as eighty-seven years before that.

Though Evelyn Dunphy considered herself an artist from age five, she dated the true beginning of her watercoloring to July 1996, when she turned fifty-six and traveled to Moosehead Lake. From her campsite, at Lily Bay, her canoe, and Mount Kineo, she painted various views.

The month prior to her first trip to Katahdin, she had explored higher latitudes. Boarding the freighter *Northern Ranger* at St. Anthony, on the northern tip of Newfoundland, she traveled the Labrador coast as far north as Nain before returning to St. Anthony mid-September. "I would stand on the deck of the ship as it plowed through the Labrador Sea—drawing—then run down to my room and paint as fast as I could," she wrote. While the ship traversed the 120-mile-long Lake Melville from east to west, stopping at ports Happy Valley and Goose Bay, she painted the Mealy Mountains (4,300 feet) along the southern shore.

In August 2004, she went to Japan. Stopping in Hakone on September 5, she drove up Mount Komaga-take to a lookout. There she had time for two paintings of Mount Fuji before it disappeared in clouds. Her *Cloud Rising Over Mt. Fuji* was featured in "Showcase of Master Painters of the US" in *International Artists Magazine*, January/February 2005. Nine days before, on August 27, she had stood atop the 12,389-foot Fuji itself, having walked up in eight and a half hours with an overnight stop at station two.

Since her first Katahdin visit, Dunphy has painted the mountain in all seasons. In March 2005, she arrived at Katahdin Lake Wilderness Camps with its owner, Al Cooper, on an antiquated snowmobile. She brought food, a sleeping bag, and paints. She stayed in a small cabin, with wood stove, chair, and cot, living as simply as Thoreau at Walden— she had read *Walden* and *The Maine Woods*. Early one morning, she snowshoed across the frozen lake to begin what became *Katahdin from the Deadwater*. Her pastel *Spring Break* and watercolor *March Thaw* also resulted from this trip. In her home studio she added one snowflake at a time to complete *Snow Falling on Katahdin*.

After Dunphy's talk to the Topsham students, they made their own paintings of the mountain. These became cards, which were sold for the benefit of Katahdin Lake. Many artists, including Dunphy, auctioned their works to raise funds to save the lake from development pressures. In December 2006, Katahdin Lake with 4,000 acres was added to Baxter State Park.

## NOTES

### Chapter One

1. In addition to these four trips to Maine, Thoreau made two more. He gave two lectures in Portland. The first was on March 21, 1849; see Walter Harding, *The Days of Henry Thoreau* (1970), 238. The second was on January 15, 1851; see John F. Jaques, "An Enthusiastic Newspaper Account of Thoreau's Second Lecture . . . ," *American Literature*, November 1968, 385–391. Further research may reveal other visits, but at present I am aware of only these six.
2. William Ellery Channing, *Thoreau: The Poet-Naturalist* (Boston: Roberts Brothers, 1873), 319.
3. See Walter Harding, "A Check List of Thoreau's Lectures," *Bulletin of the New York Public Library*, February 1948, 78–87.
4. See Joseph J. Moldenhauer's "History of the Text," *The Maine Woods* (Princeton University Press, 1972), 355–367, which elaborates considerably on this brief background of the genesis of *The Maine Woods*.
5. William Howarth and Farrell Grehan give a taste of Thoreau's major trips, including Maine, in their stimulating photographic essay in *National Geographic*, March 1981, 348–387.
6. Letter, Thoreau to H. G. O. Blake, January 1, 1859, in Walter Harding and Carl Bode, eds., *The Correspondence of Henry David Thoreau* (New York: New York University Press, 1974), 538.
7. It appears in "Ktaadn" thirty-three times, in "Chesuncook" thirty-five times, and in "The Allegash and East Branch" forty-five times, for a total of 113.
8. Dag Hammarskjöld, *Markings*, trans. by Leif Sjoberg and W. H. Auden (New York: Alfred A. Knopf, 1966), 58.
9. Thoreau's Maine relatives all descended from Henry's father's sister, Nancy Thoreau, who in 1810 married Caleb C. Billings and settled in Bangor, Maine. In 1832, Rebecca Billings married George A. Thatcher. See Leonard Kleinfeld, "Thoreau's Maine Relatives," *Thoreau Society Bulletin*, Winter 1979, 5.

    For more on George Thatcher, see Richard S. Sprague, "Companions to Katahdin: Henry David Thoreau and George A. Thatcher of Bangor," *Thoreau Journal Quarterly*, January 1980, 41–65. I do not accept Professor Sprague's assumption that Thoreau did not spend the night of July 22, 1857, at the Thatchers' while he was in Bangor.
10. I have adopted Thoreau's spelling of his guide's last name. Fannie Hardy Eckstorm used Attien and Attean in her books *Penobscot Man* and *Old John Neptune*, respectively. The Penobscot historian Glenn Starbird Jr. informed me that "Attean" is the modern form.

**Chapter Two**

1. Before joining Thoreau for this trip, Edward Sherman Hoar (1823–1893) practiced law in California (1850–1857). Like Thoreau, he was a native of Concord, a graduate of Harvard (1844), and a botanist. He attended, but did not graduate from, Harvard Law School. New York State admitted him to the bar in 1848. He has no biographer as yet, but Elizabeth Maxfield Miller of Concord, an authority on the Hoars, has helped me to learn about him.

   Thoreau's *The Maine Woods* gives the best portrait of Joe Polis, who can be understood using the suggested readings in Chapter 11.

2. Sanders Store, Inc. used to be located at this site. The store was owned by D. T. Sanders & Son, Inc. (and known by that name) until January 31, 1981, when the president of the company, Harry A. Sanders III, sold it to Roy Williams and Mel Sanborn.

   Harry A. Sanders III is the great-grandson of the founder of the business, David T. Sanders (1836–1910), the son of an English immigrant. David Sanders came to Greenville in 1852. In 1857, the year of Thoreau's second visit, he joined Shaw, Barton & Company, a firm he served for twenty-one years. In 1878, the partners established separate companies, with David Sanders building his store in its present location. Judith Sanders Sanborn, daughter of Harry A. Sanders III and a fifth-generation employee of the company, has supplied this history.

   I am curious to know whether Thoreau visited the store on July 23, 1857, when he stayed overnight in Greenville. Harry A. Sanders III claims that Thoreau was outfitted there. (See an interview with him conducted by William Pohl in *Down East*, July 1980.) I doubt that he was. I am still trying to determine whether the store was in existence then. Even if it was, Thoreau's schedule—arriving at 8:30 p.m. and departing the next morning at 4:00—permitted little time to shop.

3. Thoreau also traveled Moosehead Lake from Greenville to Northeast Carry and back in 1853. These trips were by steamer, whose course was between Deer and Sugar islands to the Kineo Hotel. This way, which appears more direct on a map, is in reality close to the same length as his later voyage. I prefer Thoreau's 1857 route for the same reason his guide did: it provides more protection from the wind.

4. Squaw Point may not be the exact place he stopped. Clearly, his description designates a location somewhere on this protrusion of land opposite Deer Island.

5. There are four storage dams on Moosehead Lake: Brassua Dam (1923), West Outlet Dam (1949), East Outlet Dam (1955), First Roach Pond Dam (1979).

6. Charles T. Jackson, *Second Annual Report of the Geology of the Public Lands* (1838), Mr. Hodge's Report, 59.

7. Charles T. Jackson, *Second Report on the Geology of the State of Maine* (1838), 125. Today the difference between normal lake level (1,029 feet) and mountain summit (1,806 feet) is 777 feet. In 1838, Jackson calculated the lake's surface to be 960 feet above sea level (see his *Third Annual Report on the Geology of the State of Maine*, 1839, 40). He

never reported climbing Mount Kineo. Probably he decided not to cover the same ground as his assistant, Hodge, but I find it hard to imagine his resisting closer examination of such a prominent geological feature.

8. Charles T. Jackson, *Second Annual Report on the Geology of Public Lands* (1838), 58.

9. I do not know when this fire occurred. F. S. Davenport stated that the railroad was there in 1861, but gone three years later. Since he could not find anyone to tell him when the fire happened, he concluded that it was in 1862 or 1863. See his "Some Pioneers of Moosehead, Chesuncook, and Millinocket," *The Northern*, June 1922, 4. A. G. Hempstead repeated Davenport's dates in his *The Penobscot Boom* (1931), 54–56. I wonder why Thoreau did not use the railroad again in 1857 when he returned: that year he and Hoar had to tote their gear, even going back for a second load, while Polis portaged the birch. (187–188)

10. Samuel Hinckley owned this clearing and lived here from 1847 to 1854, according to F. S. Davenport, in *The Northern*, June 1922, 5. The Indian encampment was located about one-quarter mile east of where the road meets the West Branch, I believe.

11. See Jackson, *Second Report on the Geology of the State of Maine* (1838), 125. Thoreau quoted Jackson (175–176). Dr. Arthur J. Boucot informed me that this is not the largest mass, not even in Maine. The Traveler Mountain rhyolite in the northern part of Baxter State Park is more extensive, for example. Hornstone, Dr. Boucot explained, is an eighteenth- and nineteenth-century term, no longer used by geologists; it means "stone whose appearance resembles animal horns."

12. In 1895, C. C. Willoughby discovered the Indian workshops at Kineo. Although they were damaged by water, which had risen to a new level because of the dam, enough evidence remained for him to relate their history (see Further Reading).

### Chapter Three

1. In 1981, Mr. Johnston was still driving the star route of Rockwood. There was a post office at the north end of the Carry. Established in 1889, it was still in existence in 1928 when A. G. Hempstead visited; see his *The Penobscot Boom* (1931), 54–55.

2. Later Hubbard's investigation revealed still another name, *Peskebegat*, meaning "branch of a dead-water" or "split or divided lake." See his *Woods and Lakes of Maine* (1971), 37, 208–209.

3. I am indebted to my friend Craig Greene for the identification of these plants.

4. Alfred G. Hempstead, *The Penobscot Boom* (1931), 140–141.

5. Pine Stream was a natural tributary when Thoreau visited. This is no longer true. Twentieth-century dams on Chesuncook Lake caused the expansion of Pine Stream's mouth for about a mile, I estimate. In 1912, a dam was built 4.5 miles up Pine Stream; this created Pine Stream Flowage, a four-mile-long deadwater, and obviously affected the flow on the stream's lower portion. This dam had since been destroyed. See Alfred G. Hempstead, *The Penobscot Boom* (1931), 142.

6. Journal of Fannie Hardy Eckstorm, "Trip Down the West Branch," August 13, 1889, Eckstorm Papers. This journal was edited and annotated by Benton J. Hatch and published in *Appalachia*, December 1949, 480–498; the quotation is from pages 483–484.

7. My friend Bob Prescott identified this clam for me.

8. Maine wildlife biologist Francis Dunn informed me that he had often witnessed this behavior; it is not rare, as I had thought.

9. Randolph L. Peterson, *North American Moose* (1978), 98.

### Chapter Four

1. The first dam at the foot of Chesuncook probably dates to 1840. This structure was repaired and improved until replaced by the 1903–1904 dam, which was succeeded by Ripogenus Dam in 1916; this is the current one. See Alfred G. Hempstead, *The Penobscot Boom* (1931), 39–44; 47–48; 117–119.

2. The first known description of the lake is that of Joseph Chadwick in 1764. Mrs. Eckstorm neither accepts this interpretation of Chesuncook nor offers another one, the Indians never giving her its meaning. See Fannie Hardy Eckstorm, "History of the Chadwick Survey . . ." in *Sprague's Journal of Maine History* (April–June 1926), 84; and her unpublished, undated paper "Chesuncook and Umbazooksus" in the Eckstorm Papers.

3. Thoreau spelled Ansel with two "l"s, while his gravestone shows only one. When Ripogenus Dam was built in 1916, the Chesuncook cemetery was moved from Graveyard Point to its present location.

4. Hubbard determined the distance at ⅛ mile, *Woods and Lakes of Maine* (1971), 63.

5. For details of this route see *AMC River Guide: Maine* 4th ed., 2008.

6. Gero lost its game refuge classification in 1959. The state owns 100 percent of a portion of the island, 50 percent undivided interest of another section, and 75 percent undivided interest in the remainder. The Bureau of Public Lands has as one of its tasks regeneration of the spruce-fir forest on the island by removing dead or damaged trees to encourage new growth.

7. The *rod* equals 16 ½ feet; a surveyor's term common in Thoreau's day, it is no longer in common usage.

8. *Walden*, edited by J. Lyndon Shanley (Princeton University Press, 1971), 217. Robert Louis Stevenson commented on Thoreau's diet: "He thought it bad economy and worthy of no true virtuoso to spoil the natural rapture of the morning with such muddy stimulants; . . ." ("Henry David Thoreau: His Character and Opinions," *Cornhill Magazine*, June 1880, 665–682; reprinted in *The Works of Robert Louis Stevenson*, vol. 4, *Familiar Studies of Men and Books*, 1922, 148; and in *Thoreau: A Century of Criticism*, edited by Walter Harding, Dallas: Southern Methodist University Press, 1954, 61.)

9. Robert P. Tristam Coffin, *Kennebec: Cradle of Americans*, 1937 (Camden, Maine: Down East Enterprise, 1973), 155.

## Chapter Five

1. Actually this is the Penobscot's East Branch watershed, as will be explained.

2. Fannie Hardy Eckstorm wondered the same thing. See her "Thoreau's 'Maine Woods'" in Walter Harding, ed., *Thoreau: A Century of Criticism* (1954), 112–113; see also Derek Conley, "Thoreau and Mud Pond Carry," *Thoreau Society Bulletin*, Fall 1980. He proposes that the trail's deterioration resulted from people-and-baggage-laden tractors.

3. Its proper name is now Carry Bog.

4. See H. K. Barrows and C. C. Babb, *Water Resources of the Penobscot River Basin, Maine* (1912), 172–173; Philip T. Coolidge, *History of the Maine Woods* (Bangor: Furbish Roberts Printing Co., 1963), 56; Fannie Hardy Eckstorm, "Lumbering in Maine," in Louise C. Hutch, ed., *Maine* (1974), 694; and Lucius L. Hubbard, *Woods and Lakes of Maine* (1971), 78. Hubbard found the second or lower dam in ruins in 1881.

5. For descriptions of these services, see David C. Smith, *A History of Lumbering in Maine 1861–1960* (1972), 395–396, 398; Alfred G. Hempstead, *The Penobscot Boom*, 125–130, 141; and Lew Dietz, *The Allagash* (1968), 226–242. Smith says the cable weighed 13 tons; Hempstead and Dietz state 14.

6. Lucius L. Hubbard, *Woods and Lakes of Maine* (1971), 76.

7. Thoreau did not identify Farrar, but Fannie Hardy Eckstorm did. See *Thoreau Society Bulletin*, Spring 1955.

8. Fannie Hardy Eckstorm, "Lumbering in Maine," in Louis C. Hatch, ed., *Maine* (1974), 695. She corrects the error of John S. Springer (*Forest Life and Forest Trees*, 1971, 209–210) that the Telos Cut was made in response to the Webster-Ashburton Treaty of 1842 with Great Britain, a version Thoreau cites (245); the canal's creation preceded the treaty. See also Lucius L. Hubbard, *Woods and Lakes of Maine* (1971), 221–223; Richard G. Wood, *A History of Lumbering in Maine, 1820–1861* (1971), 121–123; and, *The Telos Canal*, "The Evidence before the Committee on Interior Waters . . ." December 4, 1928.

9. James Russell Lowell, "A Moosehead Journal," in his *Fireside Travels* (1904), I:88, 91–92.

10. Brewster, William. *The Birds of the Lake Umbagog Region of Maine.* 1:50. Scott Sutcliffe, formerly director of New Hampshire Audubon Society's Loon Preservation Committee, told me that some farmers in Pittsburgh, New Hampshire, relied on loon flight patterns as barometers. If they flew south from Back Lake to Lake Francis, the day assuredly would be all right for cutting hay. Their passage in the other direction, however, meant inclement conditions, and "no haying."

11. *Walden*, edited by J. Lyndon Shanley (Princeton University Press, 1971), 235.

## Chapter Six

1. Lucius L. Hubbard, *Woods and Lakes of Maine* (1971), 198. I am still trying to determine where "Webster" came from.

2. Journal of Fannie Hardy Eckstorm, "Trip Down the East Branch via North East Carry," September 4, 1888, Eckstorm Papers.

3. Thoreau confused his directions here; he meant the northern side of Webster Brook. Also, their camp was not adjacent to Grand Pitch, but above the rapids which precede the cascade. Polis could not have shot these rapids in his canoe.

4. This curious diversion, called Webster Carry, was based on preference, not necessity. Polis left Webster Brook because he did not consider it navigable. The portion below Grand Pitch, however, had been passable since the completion of Telos Dam and Cut in 1842. Both routes were used. In October 1882, explorer George Witherle crossed from the East Branch to Webster Brook and back via Webster Carry (see his "Excursions North of Katahdin," *Appalachia*, December 1883, 229–230). In September 1888, Mrs. Eckstorm's guide, George Leonard, portaged around Grand Pitch and re-entered Webster Brook (see her Journal, "Trip Down the East Branch . . . ").

5. Helen Cruickshank, *Thoreau on Birds* (1964), 184–185; and, letter, Helen Cruickshank, November 13, 1979, Rockledge, Florida, to author, Keene, New Hampshire, personal papers. Mrs. Cruickshank readily admits that her conclusion may be incorrect.

### Chapter Seven

1. Apparently, hawks so devastated the game that nothing was left for hunters, who disappointedly termed the area depleted. See Hubbard, *Woods and Lakes of Maine* (1971), 200. Here Hubbard's spelling of the lakes was Matagamook and Matagamooksis; his *Guide* (1893), 137–138, referred to them as Matangamook and Matangamooksis. The Coffin map (1835) designated the eastern lake Matagamon and the western one as part of the East Branch. The 1833 "Survey Map of Maine" by Z. Bradley and Edwin Rose labeled them Matagamon and Metagamonsis (State Archives, State Cultural Building, Augusta, Maine). They are also called First and Second Lake, respectively.

2. This length is given by Barrows and Babb, *Water Resources of the Penobscot River Basin, Maine* (USGPO, 1912), 173. Obviously, when it is applied to 1857 it is an estimate, since the exact water level then was unknown. Farrar's and Hubbard's *Guide* (1889, 247; 1893, 137) stated that this thoroughfare was four or five miles long, which is exaggerated, I believe.

3. East Branch Pond is the source in the opinion of the Board of Geographic Names, based on the similarity of the two names. Stink Pond and small ponds in T7, R11, WELS are given as the source in *State of Maine: Fourth Annual Report: State Water Storage Commission, 1913* (Waterville: Sentinel Publishing Co., 1914), 137.

4. At this time there was a U.S. Post Office on the east side of Matagamon. Twice weekly mail was carried between Shin Pond and the lake by donkeys. A more direct route, Grand Lake Road, was built later, in the 1930s, by the Civilian Conservation Corps.

5. It is also referred to as Ledge Island. For a partial history of the negotiations to name it for Thoreau, see *Thoreau Journal Quarterly*, 1969: January, 20–22; July, 32; October, 30; 1970: January, 29; April, 30; July, 24.

6. Fannie Hardy Eckstorm believed that Polis's designation was a misnomer. See Avery, "The Dead-Water Mountains," *The Maine Naturalist*, April 1930, 3n.

7. Asa Gray, *Manual of Botany* (New York: G. P. Putnam & Co., 1856, second edition), 423. Gray distinguished only the black and white spruce and postulated that the three spruces were "mere forms of one species."

8. A fourth species, pitch pine, *Pinus rigida*, is also native to Maine, but its range does not extend this far north. Thoreau does not mention its presence in this area.

9. George H. Witherle, "An Autumn Visit to the Sourdnahunk Mountains and Katahdin." *Appalachia*, December 1884, 32.

10. In 1980, Great Northern informed me that, while jack pines grow on their timberlands, they do not harvest them.

### Chapter Eight

1. Eckstorm, "History of the Chadwick Survey . . ." *Sprague's Journal of Maine History* (April-June 1926), 67.

2. I have shot this rapid of three low pitches; sometimes low water forced us to lift our canoes down a tier or two.

3. Charles H. Hitchcock, "Geology of the Wild Lands," *Sixth Annual Report of the Secretary of the Maine Board of Agriculture. 1861*, 401; and Hubbard's *Guide* (1893), 141.

4. Charles E. Hamlin, "Routes to Ktaadn," *Appalachia*, December 1881, 321.

5. David C. Smith, *A History of Lumbering in Maine 1861–1960* (Orono: University of Maine Press, 1972), 80.

6. Edward Everett Hale, "An Early Ascent of Katahdin," *Appalachia,* April 1901, 282.

7. J. K. Laski, "Dr. Young's Botanical Expedition to Mount Katahdin," *The Maine Naturalist*, June 1927, 42–43.

8. G. L. Goodale, "Botanical Notes on the New Lands," *Sixth Annual Report of the Secretary of the Maine Board of Agriculture. 1861*, 362.

9. This name has a variety of forms. Thoreau used Nickatow (18, 323) and Nickertow (287), and cited others (324). I have adopted the spelling of Fannie Hardy Eckstorm; see her *Indian Place-Names of the Maine Coast* (1974), 63. The 1951 USGS Millinocket, Quadrangle gives "Nicatou."

10. "The Old Fisk House at Medway," *Thoreau Journal Quarterly*, October 1971, 30–31. Photograph of the Fiske home. My thanks to Mrs. Judy Fiske Theriault of East Millinocket, who identified Benjamin Nutting Fiske (1815–1902), her great-great-grandfather. Her family Bible shows his last name with and without an "e."

### Chapter Nine

1. Thoreau identified these two men as Lowel[l] and Raish in his 1846 journal-workbook in the Berg Collection, New York Public Library. See Moldenhauer's introduction to *The Illustrated Maine Woods*, xiii. Richard S. Sprague believed that the former was definitely Charles

Lowell, Thatcher's brother-in-law, and that the latter was possibly Horatio P. Blood. See his "Companions to Katahdin . . . " *Thoreau Journal Quarterly*, January 1980, 63, n 4.

2. Thoreau called Schoodic Stream, Little Schoodic River. McCauslin's property is identified on the survey map of Township A, Range 7 (scale one inch equals sixty rods or one-half mile), dated January 26, 1906, prepared for Great Northern. I am indebted to Dorothy B. Laverty for providing me with a copy of this map.

3. See Jackson's *Second Annual Report on the Geology of the Public Lands* (1838), 11 *ff.*

4. Hodge did not mention Fowler, but I believe that he was the one who provided the oxen. See "Mr. Hodge's Report" in Jackson, *Second Annual Report on the Geology of the Public Lands* (1838), 52.

5. Though contemporaries, Thoreau and Church never met. The twentieth-century Church family started a tradition that the artist was inspired to go to Katahdin from reading Thoreau's "Ktaadn" essay, which first appeared in 1848. John Wilmerding supports this claim.

6. Letter, F. E. Church, October 3, 1885, Hudson, New York, to A. C. Goodman, Hartford, Connecticut, Church Manuscripts, Olana.

7. Letter, L. P. Church, n.d., Hudson, New York to Bird F. Cole, Treasurer, County of Penobscot, in reply to Cole's of August 7, 1934, Church MSS, Olana.

8. For a discussion of these names, see Fanie Hardy Eckstorm's letter of December 27, 1941, reprinted in H. Walter Leavitt, *Katahdin Skylines*, 13.

### Chapter Ten

1. In a short distance, Thoreau tells of their "recrossing this stream." (56) This movement appears to be a mistake, because it places them on the side farthest from the mountain. Possibly what they forded was a logan, or backwater, of Abol Stream. Canoeing up the Abol on August 20, 1889, Fannie Hardy Eckstorm related that she "had to wade across the stream in order to" gain access to the Katahdin trail, "and all our things had to be lugged twenty rods across a logan." (See her journal in *Appalachia*, December 1949, 493.) A "recrossing" also implies a prior one. I believe that Thoreau counted their row across Abol Stream as their first crossing. When this occurred depends upon where they camped. If they spent the night north of Abol Stream, they passed its mouth on September 6; if they slept south of Abol, they went over to its other side in their bateau on the morning of the seventh.

2. For Eckstorm's criticism see her essay on "Thoreau's 'Maine Woods'" in *Thoreau: A Century of Criticism*, edited by Walter Harding, 108–109; for her ascent of Katahdin see her journal in *Appalachia*, December 1949, 492–496.

3. Rev. Joseph Blake also went this way in August 1836 (bad weather forced him to turn back at the Tableland), as did the teams of British and American surveyors in 1819 and 1820, the second and third recorded ascents.

4. I rather suspect, but cannot prove, that Jackson disclosed his Katahdin experience to Thoreau before September 1846. The Jackson-Thoreau relationship needs further research. For our present knowledge of it, see Joseph J. Moldenhauer, *The Illustrated Maine Woods*, xiii–xiv.

5. Thoreau incorporated his Saddleback essay into the "Tuesday" chapter of his first book, *A Week on the Concord and Merrimack Rivers*, 1849, which was republished by Princeton University Press in 1980, Carl F. Hovde, editor. The above quotation appears on pp. 182–183 of the Princeton edition. For the details of this trip, see Thomas Woodson, "Thoreau's Excursion to the Berkshires and Catskills." *ESQ: A Journal of the American Renaissance*, Second Quarter 1975, 82–92.

6. Letter, Thoreau to H. G. O. Blake, November 16, 1857, in Walter Harding and Carl Bode, eds. *The Correspondence of Henry David Thoreau* (1974), 498.

7. Percival P. Baxter, "Baxter State Park . . . ," *Portland Sunday Telegram*, November 30, 1941, Section C, page 1.

8. William D. Williamson, *The History of the State of Maine* (Hallowell: Glazier, Masters & Co., 1832), I, 91. Williamson was also an attorney and politician, a member of Congress and acting Governor of Maine.

9. Black spruce is now properly called *Picea mariana*.

10. Jackson, *Second Annual Report of the Geology of the Public Lands* (1838), 18.

11. The plant collection of Edward E. Hale has not been located in the Herbaria of the Arnold Arboretum and Gray Herbarium, Harvard University. I am indebted to Norton G. Miller, Associate Professor of Biology and Associate Curator, for the search. Nor does the "List of the Writings of Dr. Asa Gray" in the *American Journal of Science*, 1888, vol. 36, pp. 3–42, reveal any work on this subject.

### Chapter Eleven

1. Thoreau's description matches this hotel, which he does not identify by name. It was built in 1830 by James Penly and George Wallace, and bought in 1835 by Asa Smith, one of the town's prominent residents. See *History of Penobscot County* (1882), 895, and H. F. Walling, "Topographical Map of the County of Penobscot" (1859).

2. See Fannie Hardy Eckstorm, "History of the Chadwick Survey . . . ," *Sprague's Journal of Maine History* (April–June 1926), 82.

3. Thoreau's search was a precursor to that of archeologist Warren K. Moorehead; see his *Report on the Archaeology of Maine* (1922), 224–226.

4. I am indebted to Glenn Starbird Jr., tribal historian of the Penobscots, for the identity of this island, which *The Maine Woods* does not specify.

5. For details of this route see Fannie Hardy Eckstorm, "History of the Chadwick Survey . . . " *Sprague's Journal of Maine History* (April–June 1926), 80.

6. I do not know whether Joe Aitteon's body was returned from Shad Pond (see Chapter 9), but Mr. Starbird suspects that it was.

7. Fannie Hardy Eckstorm, *Indian Place-Names* (1974), 1–2. Thoreau learned "Rocky River" (141, 321), which Mrs. Eckstorm believed too vague to depict the hundred-foot drop between these two cities.

8. The Veazie home still stands on Route 2.

9. This point was also called *Negas* or *Negew*, which Fannie Hardy Eckstorm, in *Indian Place-Names* (1974), 22–25, suggests may mean "cut across, short cut," since Indians surmounted the falls below and above the bend (neither are extant) by portaging over the neck, a tough carry judging by the topography.

10. In 1895 street numbers were changed; the Thatcher house is now number 95. It is incorrectly cited as number 93 in Earle G. Shettleworth Jr., *Bangor Historic Resources Inventory* (Maine Historic Preservation Commission, 1975); there is no number 93 Essex Street, I found. My thanks to architectural historian Deborah Thompson of Bangor for her identification of this house.

    Thatcher moved within Bangor, for in 1848 he lived on Union Street and after 1870 on Adams Street, where Thoreau's sister, Sophia, lived from 1873 to her death in 1876. The Adams Street residence, shown on the map of the city in the *Atlas of Penobscot County* (1875), was recently demolished.

11. Fannie Hardy Eckstorm identified the others as William H. Staples of Patten, "Lane" and "Lunt, of Orono." (See *Thoreau Society Bulletin*, Spring 1955.) Hiram Lewis Leonard (1831–1907) was twenty-six, not thirty, when he met Thoreau. For more on his life, see Victor A Schlich, "The Bamboo Man of Bangor," *Down East*, May 1979, 45–47 (article mistakenly puts Thoreau-Leonard meeting in the 1870s); and Martin J. Keane, *Classic Rods and Rodmakers* (New York: Winchester Press, 1976), 29–49. Keane quotes *The Maine Woods*.

12. Charles T. Jackson, *Second Annual Report on the Geology of the Public Lands* (1838), 21.

13. George H. Stone, *The Glacial Gravels of Maine and Their Associated Deposits* (1899), 105. Curiously, Hitchcock did not mention this segment, though his report disclosed seventeen horsebacks within the state (see *Preliminary Report upon the Natural History and Geology of the State of Maine*, 1861, 271–274). Stone incorrectly assumed that none of the geologists before him noticed this esker, when in fact Jackson had. The first record of its existence is not Thoreau's, then, as Stone leads us to believe.

### Afterword

1. On April 1, 1992, I received a letter from Irvin C. "Buzz" Caverly Jr., Director of Baxter State Park from 1982 to 2005, who informed me that after nearly a half-century of service, Oliver and Della Cobb retired in the early 1960s.

## FURTHER READING

### Chapter I

### Thoreau Biography

Harding, Walter. *The Days of Henry Thoreau.* (New York: Alfred A. Knopf, 1965). Dr. Harding (1917–1996) was the preeminent authority on Thoreau.

Krutch, Joseph Wood. *Henry David Thoreau.* (New York: William Morrow & Company, Inc., 1974).

Lebeaux, Richard. *Young Man Thoreau.* (Amherst: University of Massachusetts Press, 1977). An Eriksonian interpretation. For an excellent review of this see Leo Marx, "The Two Thoreaus," *The New York Review*, October 26, 1978, 37–44.

Wagenknecht, Edward. *Henry David Thoreau: What Manner of Man?* (Amherst: University of Massachusetts Press, 1981). A delightful study, well worth reading.

### Thoreau Criticism

Christie, John Aldrich. *Thoreau as World Traveler.* (New York: Columbia University Press, 1965).

Cook, Reginald L. *Passage to Walden.* 1949. (New York: Russell & Russell, 1966).

Eckstorm, Fannie Hardy. "Thoreau's 'Maine Woods'" in Walter Harding, ed., *Thoreau: A Century of Criticism.* (Dallas: Southern Methodist University Press, 1954). 103–117. For a rejoinder to Eckstorm's critique, see Mary P. Sherwood, "Fanny Eckstorm's Bias," *The Massachusetts Review*, Autumn 1962, 139–147. For more on Thoreau as a birder, see Bradford Torrey's "Introduction" to *The Journal of Henry D. Thoreau*, 1906. (New York: Dover Publications, Inc., 1962), I: xliii–xlvii; and Walter Harding's reply in the foreword to the 1962 edition of *The Journal*, vii.

Paul, Sherman. *The Shores of America: Thoreau's Inward Exploration.* 1958. (Urbana: University of Illinois Press, 1972). Contains an analysis of *The Maine Woods.*

### Maine

Clark, Charles E. *Maine: A Bicentennial History.* (New York: W. W. Norton & Company, 1977).

Saltonstall Jr., Richard. *Maine Pilgrimage.* (Boston: Little, Brown and Company, 1974). The author follows Thoreau's route in Maine while reading *The Maine Woods.*

### Chapter 2

### Greenville

*Moosehead Souvenir Booklet.* Greenville, Maine. 1976. Brief accounts of people, places, and pursuits in the area.

True, Emma J., ed. *History of Greenville.* (Augusta, Maine: The Augusta Press. 1936).

### Moosehead Lake Travelers

Here is a sampling of other firsthand accounts of Moosehead Lake and the Maine woods.

Hardwick, M. E., and E. L. Sampson, "Canoeing the Penobscot," *Appalachia*, May 1890, 34-45. Two female members of the Appalachian Mountain Club write of their month, August 1889, in the Maine woods with four others, two of whom were Old Town Indian guides. After crossing Moosehead by steamer, they descended the Penobscot West Branch in three canoes of canvas, "which in these waters has superseded birch almost entirely," making stops at Lobster Lake for the night and Chesuncook Farm for "some milk and half a lamb." From Abol Stream, where they camped for a week, on 13 August they walked to "a mile or so below" the "South Slide," where they camped. The next morning they ascended Abol Slide to the Tableland and went on to the summit in three and a half hours. "Ktaadn," for them, was "too stern and forbidding" to "feel any affection for." Beginning their descent at eleven o'clock, they returned to their Abol-West Branch camp by supper time. They made no reference to their predecessors: Thoreau, Church, Winthrop.

Hubbard, Lucius L. *Woods and Lakes of Maine.* (Somersworth: New Hampshire Publishing Company, [1883] 1971). His 1881 trip was from Greenville down the Allagash to the St. John. Hubbard (1849–1934) was a Boston lawyer who changed his career to geology, becoming the State Geologist of Michigan in 1893.

Lanman, Charles. "Moosehead Lake and the Kennebeck." In *Letters from a Landscape Painter.* (Boston: James Monroe and Company, 1845). Lanman (1819–1895), a writer, amateur explorer, artist, and Thoreau contemporary, visited northern Maine in the 1830s.

Lowell, James Russell. "A Moosehead Journal." *Fireside Travels.* In *The Complete Writings of James Russell Lowell.* 16 vols. (Boston: Houghton Mifflin & Company, 1904), I: 71–117. Lowell (1819–1891) enjoyed a distinguished reputation as a poet and prose writer in the nineteenth century. As editor of the *Atlantic Monthly*, he published Thoreau's "Chesuncook" in June 1858.

Lucid, Robert F., ed., *The Journal of Richard Henry Dana, Jr.* (Cambridge: Belknap Press of Harvard University Press, 1968). 3 vols. 2:245–259. Dana, a Boston attorney and the author of *Two Years Before the Mast* (1840), came to Moosehead Lake in August 1851. Staying at Kineo House, he made two ascents of the mountain, sailed the lake in a sloop, hunted moose from a birch-bark canoe, and captured all of this in his journal.

Montresor, John. "Journal of a Scout, 1761." In Kenneth Roberts, ed., *March on Quebec: Journals of Members of Arnold's Expedition.* (New York: Doubleday, Doran & Company, Inc., 1938), 1–24. An engineer in the British Army, Montresor (1736–1799) mapped the waterways, including Moosehead Lake, between the St. Lawrence and the Atlantic Ocean in 1761. Thoreau read Montresor's diary.

Packard, Hanscom. "Mount Kineo." *New England Magazine*, August 1903, 727–737. "Moosehead Lake is at once the greatest and the most beautiful of the many hundreds of sheets of water in the Maine forests," Packard proclaimed. His account draws on James Russell Lowell, not Thoreau.

Trowbridge, John Townshend. "A Trip to Moosehead Lake in 1849." *Down East*, July 1961, 40 *ff.* An abstract of the original, which appeared in a Boston newspaper, *The Olive Branch*, starting on August 9, 1849.

### Nineteenth-Century Guides

No guidebooks to the Maine woods were available for Thoreau's use. These popular references encouraged many to see the region for themselves later, though.

Farrar, Captain Charles A. J. *Farrar's Illustrated Guide Book to Moosehead Lake . . . .* 9th ed. (Boston: Lee & Shepard, 1889). He also published other guides to the area, such as *Down the West Branch.*

Hubbard, Lucius L. *Hubbard's Guide to Moosehead Lake and Northern Maine.* 5th ed. (Cambridge: Published by the Author, 1893). This apparently was the last edition. The first edition was titled *Summer Vacations at Moosehead Lake and Vicinity*, as was the second edition; both were published in Boston by A. Williams and Company in 1879 and 1880, respectively. For more see Benton L. Hatch, compiler, "Lucius Lee Hubbard's Map of Northern Maine, 1879–1929; A Check List," *Appalachia* (June 1951): 453–464.

Way, John M., Jr., *Guide to Moosehead Lake, and Northern Maine with Map.* (Boston: Bradford & Anthony, 1874). This was the first guide and sportsman's map published to the Moosehead Lake region.

### Contemporary Guides

Fiske, John, ed. *AMC River Guide: Maine.* 4th ed. (Boston: Appalachian Mountain Club Books, 2008).

*Maine Mountain Guide.* 9th ed. (Boston: Appalachian Mountain Club Books, 2005).

### Thoreau's Maps of Maine

Thoreau consulted the following maps of Maine:

Coffin, George W. "A Plan of the Public Lands in the State of Maine Surveyed under Instructions from the Commissioners and Agents of the States of Massachusetts and Maine." August 1, 1835. Thoreau carried this map with him in 1853 and 1857, and made corrections on it. His copy is in the Concord Free Public Library, Concord, Massachusetts (without date, scale, or cartographer). Others are in the Maine State Library, Augusta (Boston: Pendleton's Lithography, 1835), and the Public Record Office, London, England (reference: CO. 700/21).

Colton, Joseph Hutchins. "Railroad and Township Map of the State of Maine. . . . " 1855. A copy is in the Maine State Library, Augusta.

Greenleaf, Moses. "Map of the State of Maine. . . . " 1829. Thoreau traced a copy of this map to take with him in 1846; he found it "a labyrinth of errors." (15) Various editions of Greenleaf's maps are in the Maine State Library, Augusta, the Maine Historical Society, Portland, and the Library of Congress, Washington, D.C.

Along with his maps, Greenleaf published two books (Thoreau does not mention them), which provided needed information about Maine's natural resources: *A Statistical View of the District of Maine* (Boston: Cummings and Hilliard, 1816) and *A Survey of the State of Maine* (Portland: Shirley and Hyde, 1829; reprint edition, Augusta: Maine State Museum, 1970).

For more on Greenleaf (1777–1834), see Hayden L. V. Anderson, "Penobscot Waterways. . . . " *Maine Historical Society Quarterly,* (Summer 1979): 21–46; and, Edgar Crosby Smith, ed., *Moses Greenleaf, Maine's First Map Maker* (Bangor: De Burians, 1902). Biographical sketches of Greenleaf appear in Louis C. Hatch, ed., *Maine* (1974): 896–897; Lew Dietz, *The Allagash* (1968): 47–54; the reprint edition of his *Survey, supra.*; and the *DAB* and *ANB.*

Stowell, Robert F. *A Thoreau Gazetteer.* William L. Howarth, ed. (Princeton, N.J.: Princeton University Press, 1970). This features sections of the Coffin and Colton maps.

### Maine Woods Landforms—Mount Kineo

Boucot, Arthur J. *Geology of the Moose River and Roach River Synclinoria, Northwestern Maine.* (Augusta: Department of Economic Development, 1969). And his *Stratigraphy of the Moose River Synclinorium, Maine.* Washington, D.C.: USGPO, 1961, U.S. Geological Survey Bulletin 1111-E.

Ferland Jr. Durward J. *Kineo: Splendor and Silence.* (Greenville, Maine: Moosehead Communications, 1996). This is a mostly pictorial history of the Kineo hotel complex.

Forbes, Charles B. "Mt. Kineo, Maine." *Appalachia.* (June 1967): 521–527. A general social and natural history of the mountain.

Jackson, Charles T. *First Report on the Geology of the State of Maine.* (Augusta: Smith & Robinson, Printers to the State, 1837). And his other reports: *Second Report on the Geology of the State of Maine.* (Augusta: Luther Severance, Printer, 1838). *Third Annual Report on the Geology of the State of Maine.* (Augusta: Smith & Robinson, Printers to the State, 1839). *First Report on the Geology of the Public Lands in the State of Maine.* (Boston: Dutton and Wentworth, Printers to the State, 1837). *Second Annual Report on the Geology of the Public Lands Belonging to the Two States of Maine and Massachusetts.* (Augusta: Luther Severance, Printer, 1838). Thoreau read these descriptions of Maine's landscape and natural history, and I frequently draw upon them for information for this guide.

Macdougall, Walter M. "Kineo." *Down East.* June 1976, 62–67; 85–89. A discussion of the Kineo Hotel from its initial construction to the present, with historical photographs.

Moorehead, Warren K. *A Report on the Archaeology of Maine.* (Andover, Mass.: The Andover Press, 1922). For Moosehead Lake see pages 215 *ff.* Moorehead (1866–1939) was field director of the archaeological survey of New England; his explorations of Maine were conducted from 1912 to 1920.

Smith, Edward S. C. "The Igneous Rock of Mt. Kineo and Vicinity." *American Journal of Science.* (November 1925): 437–444.

Sprague, John Francis. "Mount Kineo and the Maine Summer Resort Industry." *Sprague's Journal of Maine History* (May 1914): 10–16. Lists all the owners and landlords of Kineo from 1840 to 1914.

Willoughby, Charles Clark. *Antiquities of the New England Indians.* (Cambridge, Mass.: Peabody Museum of American Archaeology and Ethnology, Harvard University, 1935). Especially pages 122–124. His earlier article contained much of the same information: "Prehistoric Workshops at Mt. Kineo, Maine." *The American Naturalist* (March 1901): 213–216. Dr. Willoughby (1857–1943) served the Peabody Museum of Harvard for half a century, from 1894 until his death, and was its director form 1915 to 1928. For more on this remarkable ethnographer see Earnest A. Hooton, "Charles Clark Willoughby," *American Antiquity*, 2, 1943, 235–239.

### Chapter 3

### Maine Woods Animals
#### General

Godin, Alfred J. *Wild Mammals of New England.* (Baltimore: The Johns Hopkins University Press, 1977). Habits, appearance, and life histories of 1,100 species of mammals found in New England, with drawings of each and range maps of their distribution. An excellent work.

Seton, Ernest Thompson. *Lives of Game Animals.* (Boston: Charles T. Branford Company, [1909] 1953). Many interesting anecdotes and first-hand reports on moose and other mammals.

Also helpful are articles in *Maine Fish and Wildlife, Journal of Mammalogy, Journal of Wildlife Management, Ecology,* and the concise reports on *Mammalian Species* of the American Society of Mammalogists.

#### Thoreau's Reference

Audubon, John James, and John Bachman. *The Quadrupeds of North America.* 3 Vol. (New York: George R. Lockwood, 1849). Thoreau's library contained volume one. For moose, see II: 179–192; caribou, III: 111–124.

#### Field Guides

Murie, Olaus J. *Peterson Field Guide to Animal Tracks.* 3rd ed. (Boston: Houghton Mifflin, 2005).

Reid, Fiona. *Peterson Field Guide to Mammals of North America.* 4th ed. (Boston: Houghton Mifflin, 2006).

#### Moose

Peterson, Randolph L. *North American Moose.* 1955. (Toronto: University of Toronto Press, 1978). The definitive work on moose by the late Curator of Mammalogy of the Royal Ontario Museum, Toronto. He updated his 1955 study in two articles, "Moose: Yesterday, Today and Tomorrow," and "A Review of the General Life History of Moose," *Naturaliste Canadien,* January–April 1974, 101: 1–8, 9–21. See also his *The Mammals of Eastern Canada.* (Toronto: Oxford University Press, 1966).

Schmidt, John L., and Douglas L. Gilbert, eds. *Big Game of North America, Ecology and Management.* (Harrisburg, Penn.: Stackpole Books, 1978). An excellent article on all aspects of moose by Albert W. Franzmann, Research Biologist, Kenai Moose Research Center, Alaska, 67 *ff.*

## Chapter 4

### Chesuncook

Conaway, James, "Call of the Loon," *National Geographic Traveler*, July/August 2001, 74–82. The author's canoe trip with renowned guides Alexandra and Garrett Conover and four others from Lobster Lake down the Penobscot West Branch and Chesuncook Lake, with an overnight stay at the Chesuncook Lake House.

Curtis, Wayne, "Lodges in Rugged, Remote Maine," *The New York Times*, 1 July 1990, A17, A26.

Devenport, F. S. "Some Pioneers of Moosehead, Chesuncook and Millinocket." *The Northern* (April 1922 to March 1923). Twelve chapters. Davenport, who visited Chesuncook Lake three times in the 1860s, was apparently so impressed with Thoreau's description of Ansel Smith's that he plagiarized part of it (see August 1922).

Ford, Royal, "Spring Fever Hits the North Woods," *The Boston Globe,* 13 April 1992, 1, 10.

Gagnon, Lana. *Chesuncook Memories.* (privately printed, August 1974). The author, who first came to Chesuncook in September 1932, wrote a series of articles about her experiences which appeared in the *Moosehead Gazette* between 1963 and 1972, and are republished here. Mrs. Gagnon was one of Bert McBurnie's schoolteachers.

Montgomery, Sy, "So Quiet It Hurts," *Yankee*, October 1995, 128.

Schultz, Christine, "'There's No Place on Earth I'd Rather Live,'" *Yankee*, June 2002, 46–51.

### Muskrat

Murray, Donald M. "Thoreau and the Example of the Muskrat." *Thoreau Journal Quarterly*. (October 1978): 3–12. Murray, professor of English at Northern Illinois University and traveler of Thoreau's Maine trails, believes that the muskrat was a role model for Thoreau, a symbol of "wildness, of organic life with nature, and of stoic and unassuming courage."

See also Godin, *Wild Mammals of New England*, 130–134.

### Maine Woods Flora
#### General

Angelo, Ray. "Ledum Swamp and Labrador Tea in Concord." *The Concord Saunterer* (Spring 1979): 14–18. Angelo discovered Labrador tea in another Concord bog on August 22, 1978, confirming that it had never been extinct in the town since Thoreau's time; Ledum Swamp, however, is dead. Angelo's two guides, *Concord Area Shrubs* and *Concord Area Trees*, published by the Concord Field Station for Harvard University in 1978 and 1976, respectively, identify many plants of Maine as well.

Coon, Nelson. *Dictionary of Useful Plants*. (Emmaus, Penn.: Rodale Press, 1974). *Using Plants for Healing* (Emmaus, Penn.: Rodale Press, 1979). And, *Using Wild and Wayside Plants*. (New York: Dover Publications, Inc., 1980). (Originally published as *Using Wayside Plants*, New York: Hearthside Press, Inc., 1957.) Guides to use and preparation of herbal remedies by a leading horticulturalist.

Fernald, Merritt Lyndon, and Alfred Charles Kinsey. *Edible Wild Plants of Eastern North America*. Revised by Reed C. Collins. (New York: Harper and Row, [1943] 1958). Lists esculents by use (teas appear on pp. 24–25, and fruits on 29 *ff.*), as well as describes the purpose of each; cites Thoreau's *The Maine Woods*.

Gibbons, Euell. *Stalking the Healthful Herbs*. (New York: David McKay Company, Inc., 1966, 1975). His *Stalking the Wild Asparagus*. (New York: David McKay Company, Inc., 1962). And, Gibbons' *Euell Handbook of Edible Wild Plants*, completed by Gordon Tucker. (Virginia Beach, Va.: The Donning Company, Publishers, 1979). Gibbons probably ate more wild food than anyone in his lifetime. He writes with wit, charm, and clarity. Take his guides along.

Grieve, Maud. *A Modern Herbal*. (New York: Dover Publications, Inc., [1931] 1971. Descriptions, constituents, and medicinal action and uses are given for each plant. Gibbons is indebted to her work.

Sherwood, Mary P. "The Wild Food Hobby." *New England Wildflower Notes* of New England Wildflower Society, Framingham, Mass. (Fall 1978). A dedicated Thoreauvian, Mary Sherwood (1906–2001) argues that the wholesale collection of wild plants for food and medicine will lead to their demise. Her viewpoint should be compared with that of Gibbons, who does not "equate conservation with non-use." The forager, he believes, will not destroy his sustenance, but will preserve it.

Weiner, Michael A. *Earth Medicine, Earth Foods. Plant Remedies, Drugs, and Natural Foods of the North American Indians*. (New York: Macmillan Publishing Company, Inc., Collier Books, 1972). He gives the native uses of plants without recommending them. Cites Thoreau's *The Maine Woods*.

### Thoreau's Botanies

"Botanies, instead of being the poetry, are the prose, of flowers," Thoreau once remarked. (January 21, 1852) Not withstanding his reservations, he learned about Maine's flora from them, as well as from his field studies and from his discussions with the Indians. He found useful the below, published authorities of his day, life sketches of whom appear in the *DAB* and *ANB*.

Bigelow, Jacob. *Florula Bostoniensis*. (Boston: Cummings & Hilliard, 1814. Second edition, 1824). Third edition titled *Plants of Boston and Its Vicinity*. (Boston: Charles C. Little &

James Brown, 1840). Bigelow's, which was the standard botany of New England until Gray's, was Thoreau's first flora guide; he began using it in 1836. He also consulted Bigelow's *American Medical Botany*. 3 vol. (Boston: Dutton & Wentworth, Printers, 1846). Thoreau's library contained a copy.

Gray, Asa. *A Manual of the Botany of the Northern United States*. (Boston and Cambridge, 1848). Second edition: (New York: G. P. Putnam, 1856). Thoreau owned both editions of Gray's *Manual*; the second edition accompanied him to Maine in 1857. For more on Gray, see A. Hunter Dupree. *Asa Gray, 1810–1888*. (Cambridge: The Belknap Press of Harvard University Press, 1959).

Josselyn, John. *New-Englands Rarities Discovered: In Birds, Beasts, Fishes, Serpents, and Plants of That Country*. 1672. (Boston: Massachusetts Historical Society, 1972). And, his *An Account of Two Voyages to New-England Made During the Years 1638, 1663*. 1674. (Boston: William Veazie, 1865). Thoreau borrowed Josselyn's works from Harvard Library in 1851 and 1855; he liked the Englishman's style: "caring more to speak heartily than scientifically true." (January 9, 1855) Josselyn made two references to the interior of Maine, both of which Thoreau quotes in "Chesuncook." (141, 148) For more on these naturalists, see Philip F. Gura, "Thoreau and John Josselyn," *New England Quarterly*, December 1975, 505–518.

Michaux, Francois André. *The North American Sylva*. 3 vol. (Philadelphia: William Rutter & Co., 1871). Originally published in French between 1810–1813, Michaux's *Sylva* was translated into English by Augustus L. Hillhouse and published in Paris in four volumes, 1817–1819. The first two American editions were released from New Harmony, Indiana, in 1842 and from Philadelphia in 1852, the latter with notes by J. J. Smith. Joseph J. Mildenhauer concludes that Thoreau did not translate from the French but consulted either the Hillhouse or Smith editions for his quotation on Michaux on lumbering in "Ktaadn." (44) Thoreau's two other Michaux references in *The Maine Woods* (269, 299) are also from the *Sylva*. Thoreau quoted extensively from Michaux in his *Journal*.

### Field Guides

Adams, Herman P., et al. *Checklist of the Vascular Plants of Maine. Josselyn Botanical Society of Maine, Bulletin 13*. 3rd ed. (Orono, Maine: Maine Agricultural and Forest Experiment Station, 1995). Lists by counties all known stations of native Maine vascular plants.

Campbell, Christopher S., and Fay Hyland. *Winter Keys to Woody Plants of Maine*. (Orono, Maine: University of Maine at Orono Press, 1977). The splendid illustrations of Mary L. F. Campbell help to identify flora in any season.

Dwelley, Marilyn. *Trees and Shrubs of New England*. (Camden, Maine: Down East Books, 1980). Also her other guides by the same publisher, *Spring Wildflowers of New England*

(1973) and *Summer and Fall Wildflowers of New England* (1977), depict the flora in layman's language and color drawings.

Eastman, L. M. *Rare and Endangered Vascular Plant Species in Maine.* (Prepared by the New England Botanical Club for the U.S. Fish and Wildlife Service, Newton, Massachusetts, 1978). Cites 248 rare and endangered plants.

Harris, Stuart K., et al. *AMC Field Guide to Mountain Flowers of New England.* (Boston: Appalachian Mountain Club, 1964). Many references to plants found on Katahdin.

Johnson, Judith B. *The Heritage of Our Maine Wildflowers.* (Rockland, Maine: Courier of Maine Books, 1978). This illustrated guide is limited to herbs, for which it gives identity, history, folklore or legend, medicinal use, and edible parts.

Newcomb, Lawrence. *Newcomb's Wildflower Guide.* (Boston: Little, Brown and Co., 1989). Offers a new, less technical identification system.

Peterson, Lee. *A Field Guide to Edible Wild Plants: Eastern and Central North America.* (Boston: Houghton Mifflin, 1999). Inspired by Euell Gibbons and by Lee's father, Lee Peterson prepared this guide of more than 370 species, each with an illustration and narrative description; the latter includes habitat, use, and preparation.

Peterson, Roger Tory, and Margaret McKenny. *A Field Guide to Wildflowers of Northeastern and North-Central North America.* (Boston: Houghton Mifflin, 1968). 1,344 of Peterson's superb drawings appear in this book.

Seymour, Frank C. *The Flora of New England.* (Rutland, Vt.: Charles E. Tuttle Company, 1969). Identifies places in Maine where species are found. Technical.

### Chapter 5

### Allagash Lakes

Dietz, Lew. *The Allagash.* (New York: Holt, Rinehart and Winston, 1968). A good history of the river, with many references to Thoreau and other nineteenth-century travelers.

Eckstorm, Fannie P. Hardy. "Windbound on Chamberlain." *Forest and Stream.* November 7, 1889, 303. A natural history essay from a series of ten by the author, called "Out-of-Door Papers."

Hempstead, A. G. "A Visit to Chamberlain Farm." *The Northern*, November 1927, 14–15.

Kidney, Dorothy Boone. *Away from It All.* (Cranbury, N.J.: A. S. Barnes and Co., 1969). *A Home in the Wilderness*, same publisher, 1976. And, her *Wilderness Journal*. (Portland,

Maine: Guy Gannett Publishing Company, 1980). These books relate her experiences in the Allagash region and those of others she knew, such as the Nugents, McBurnies, Clair Desmond, and Jim Clarkson.

## Maine Woods Birds
### General

These excellent sources provide material on the birds Thoreau sighted.

Bent, Arthur Cleveland. *Life Histories of North American Birds*, 20 vol. 1919–1953. (New York: Dover Publications, Inc.) All you wanted to know about birds and more.

Bennett, Dean. *The Wilderness from Chamberlain Farm: A Story of Hope for the American Wild.* (Washington, DC: Island Press, 2001).

Brewster, William. *The Birds of the Lake Umbagog Region of Maine.* 4 parts (last part concluded by Ludlow Griscom). *Bulletin of the Museum of Comparative Zoology at Harvard College.* (Cambridge, Massachusetts, 1924–1938). Brewster (1851–1919), the father of the American Ornithologists' Union, is one of the best American bird observers and writers. His bibliography was published by the Nuttall Ornithological Club in 1951.

Palmer, Ralph S. *Handbook of North American Birds.* 3 vol. (New Haven, Conn.: Yale University Press, 1962–1988).

Palmer, Ralph S. *Maine Birds. Bulletin of the Museum of Comparative Zoology at Harvard College.* (Cambridge, Massachusetts, 1949). Historical review of Maine bird life, with extensive bibliography of authorities cited.

Terres, John K. *The Audubon Society Encyclopedia of North American Birds.* (New York: Alfred A. Knopf, 1980). By the former editor of *Audubon* and a John Burroughs Medalist. Life histories of 847 birds, marvelous color photographs—many artistic like those of brants and snow geese in flight, biographies of naturalist-ornithologists, though not Thoreau, and bibliography.

Also helpful are such ornithological journals as *The Auk, Condor, Wilson Bulletin, Audubon,* and *Maine Audubon Quarterly.*

### Thoreau on Birds

Two collections of Thoreau's bird writings have been made.

Cruickshank, Helen, ed. *Thoreau on Birds.* (New York: McGraw-Hill, 1964). A superb book by a leading ornithologist, who knows Thoreau's Maine firsthand. She comments on Thoreau's avian passages from *The Maine Woods,* as well as from his other writings.

Thoreau, Henry D. *Notes on New England Birds.* Francis H. Allen, ed. (Boston: Houghton Mifflin Co., 1910). Allen, a dedicated Thoreauvian and ornithologist, has compiled by species Thoreau's bird observations that are contained in his *Journal*, with page references to those in *The Maine Woods* and his other works. A new edition titled *Thoreau on Birds: Notes on New England Birds from the Journals of Henry David Thoreau* was published by Beacon Press of Boston in 1990.

### Thoreau's Field Guides to Birds

As Helen Cruickshank suggests, it is illuminating to read the descriptions in these early guides to American ornithology, which Thoreau used.

Audubon, John James. 8 vol. *The Birds of America, from Drawings Made in the United States and Their Territories.* (London: J. J. Audubon, 1827–1838).

Nuttall, Thomas. *A Manual of Ornithology.* 2 vol. (Boston: Hilliard, Gray & Co., 1832–1834).

Wilson, Alexander. *American Ornithology.* 9 vol. (Philadelphia: Bradford and Inskeep, 1808–1814).

### Today's Field Guides to Birds

*The Audubon Society Field Guide to North American Birds: Eastern Region.* (New York: Alfred A. Knopf, 1994). Color photographs arranged by visual characteristics; text, by habitat.

Peterson, Roger Tory. *A Field Guide to the Birds of Eastern and Central North America.* 5th ed. (Boston: Houghton Mifflin Co., 2002). Illustrations are new or redrawn by the artist, who created this identification system which is now named for him.

Vickery, Peter D. *Annotated Check List of Maine Birds.* (Falmouth, Maine: Maine Audubon Society, 1978). Concise guide to habitats and occurrence of Maine's 393 species.

### Loon

Anderson, Charles R. *The Magic Circle of Walden.* (New York: Holt, Rinehart & Winston, 1968), 193–197. An analysis of Thoreau's use of the loon in the "Brute Neighbors" chapter of *Walden.*

Armstrong, Edward A. *The Folklore of Birds.* (St. James Place, London: Collins Clear-Type Press, 1958), 62–70. Armstrong relates the loon traditions of the Shetland Islanders as rain-goose and of the Algonquin Indians as messenger of their culture-hero, Kuloskap.

Cavell, Stanley. *The Senses of Walden*. (New York: The Viking Press, 1974), 39–42. Cavell believes that Thoreau uses birds to reveal his most "intimate identifications;" the loon, he suggests, illustrates some of *Walden's* themes: insanity, change, solitude.

McPhee, John. *The Survival of the Bark Canoe*. (New York: Farrar, Straus, and Giroux, 1975), 29–31. McPhee retraces parts of Thoreau's Maine journey with bark canoe maker Henri Vaillancourt of Greenville, New Hampshire. His portrait of the loon should not be missed.

Olson, Sigurd T., and William H. Marshall. *The Common Loon in Minnesota*. (Minneapolis: University of Minnesota Press, 1952). For more on the loon's call, read this and L. L. Hubbard, *Woods and Lakes of Maine* (1971), 86–90; also Brewster's *Birds of Lake Umbagog*, I: 49–50.

Shanley, J. Lyndon. *The Making of Walden*. 1957. (University of Chicago Press. Midway Reprint, 1973), 62, 64, 76. Shanley informs us that Thoreau incorporated his loon chase, which was recorded in his *Journal* for October 8, 1852, in *Walden* for the first time in its fifth version.

Shoener, Tom. "The Lonely Yodeler of Maine Lakes." *Maine Fish and Game*. Summer 1974. General account of loon behavior.

Sutcliffe, Scott A., ed. *The Common Loon*. (New York: National Audubon Society, 1979). Proceedings of the second North American Conference on Common Loon research and management. Includes two survey reports on the status of the loon in Maine. See also Sutcliffe's "Spirit of Northern Waters," *Appalachia*, December 1979, 35–40.

## Chapter 6

### Maine Woods Birds

Consult the readings on birds given in Chapter 5.

Hardy, Manly. "Sheldrakes." *Forest and Stream*, March 25, 1899, 226. Manly Hardy (1832–1910) was born in Hampden, Maine, and died at his home in Brewer Maine. He was the father of Fannie Hardy Eckstorm; he was also a fur trapper, naturalist, and ornithologist—a recognized authority on the birds of eastern and northern Maine, a region he knew intimately. In 1912, the Rhode Island Audubon Society bought his bird collection of 3,300 species, which is still in their possession; it is housed and at times exhibited at the Roger Williams Park Museum in Providence. See Fannie Hardy Eckstorm, "Manly Hardy." *The Journal of the Maine Ornithological Society*, March 1911, 1–9.

*Manly Hardy (1832–1910): The Life and Writing of a Maine Fur-Buyer, Hunter, and Naturalist.* Compiled and introduced by William B. Krohn. (Orono: Maine Folklife Center, 2005).

## Chapter 7

### "Dead-Water Mountains"

Avery, Myron H. "The Traveler: Two Decades—Random Notes." (Augusta: The Maine Appalachian Trail Club, Inc., 1949). Reprinted from *The Lewiston Journal Magazine*, April 2 and 9, 1949. Avery's account of his climbs of Traveler Mountain in 1927 with Henry R. Buck and in 1929 with Dr. J. F. Schairer. For more on the 1927 expedition, see Henry R. Buck, "Traveler Mountain and North of Katahdin," *Appalachia*, June 1928, 13–26. A fuller record of the 1929 trip is given by Avery in "The New Route to Mr. Katahdin . . . " *In the Maine Woods*, 1928, 13–26. A fuller record of the 1929 trip is given by Avery in "The Dead-Water Mountains," *The Maine Naturalist*, April 1930, 3–19, which discusses their finding *Pinus banksiana* on Bald Mountain on August 20, 1929, pp. 10–11.

"Museum Expeditions, 1910." *Boston Society of Natural History. Museum and Library Bulletin, No. 13*, October 1910, 1–4. In the summer of 1910, Dr. J. A. Cushman and Rev. C. B. Ames collected plants from the Traveler; unfortunately, fire had destroyed much of the flora. The species located are not reported.

Witherle, George Henry. "Excursions North of Katahdin." *Appalachia*, December 1883, 222–231. In the fall of 1882, Witherle climbed several mountains in this region, specifically Hunt, Sugar Loaf, Horse, and the Traveler, whose height he calculated almost correctly. Witherle (1831–1906), of Castine, Maine, continued to explore this area until 1901, when he made his ninth and final ascent of Katahdin. His diary of these years (1880–1901), titled *Explorations West and Northwest of Katahdin in the Late Nineteenth Century* (Maine Appalachian Trail Club, Inc., 1950, 2nd ed.) was edited by Myron H. Avery (with Henry R. Buck for the first edition, undated). Both editions are in the Maine State Library at Augusta. The second edition is also in the library of the Appalachian Mountain Club in Boston. For more on Witherle, see George A. Wheeler, M.D., *History of Castine, Penobscot and Brooksville, Maine.* (Cornwall, New York: privately printed, 1923), 428–429.

### Maine Woods Flora
#### Boreal Forest

Dame, Lorin L., and Henry Brooks. *Handbook of the Trees of New England.* 1901. (New York: Dover Publications, Inc., 1972). Tells where in Maine species are found and often by whom, with references to the literature.

Fowells, H. A., comp. *Silvics of Forest Trees of the United States.* (Washington, D.C.: USGPO, 1975). Agriculture Handbook No. 271. Authoritative data on habitat and life histories of 127 species, including range maps and bibliography for each.

Hyland, Fay. *The Conifers of Maine*. (Orono: University of Maine, Cooperative Extension Service Bulletin 345. Revised, 1974). Descriptions of Maine's 16 native and five commonly introduced conifers, with statements on occurrence and uses. Illustrated and with key.

Hyland, Fay, and Barbara Hoisington. *The Woody Plants of Sphagnous Bogs of Northern New England and Adjacent Canada*. (Orono: University of Maine at Orono—Life Sciences and Agriculture Experiment Station, Bulletin 744, November 1977). Concise descriptions of 50 species with beautiful illustrations by Laurel Smith; key.

Hyland, Fay, and Ferdinand H. Steinmetz. *Trees and Other Woody Plants of Maine, Their Occurrence and Distribution*. (Thorndike, Maine: The Thorndike Press and University of Maine at Orono Press, 1978). Useful descriptions of habitats of species, with their location by county and further readings.

Mirov, Nicholas T., and Jean Hasbrouck. *The Story of Pines*. (Bloomington: Indiana University Press, 1976). This celebrated tree family has many members which have contributed to the richness of our forests.

Peattie, Donald Culross. *A Natural History of Trees of Eastern and Central North America*. (New York: Bonanza Books, 1964). Enjoyable illumination of the real and fancied history of many trees. Cites Thoreau's *The Maine Woods*. His new *A Natural History of North American Trees* (Boston: Houghton Mifflin, 2007) combines and updates this work, as well as his book on western trees.

More information about the North Woods in particular and forest ecology in general can be obtained from relevant chapters in Henry A. Gleason and Arthur Cronquist, *The Natural Geography of Plants*. (New York: Columbia University Press, 1964); Rutherford Platt, *The Great American Forest*. (Englewood Cliffs, New Jersey: Prentice-Hall, 1965); and Stephen H. Spurr and Burton V. Barnes, *Forest Ecology*. (New York: John Wiley & Sons, 1973).

### Field Guides

Harlow, William M. *Trees of the Eastern and Central United States and Canada*. (New York: Dover Publications, Inc., 1957). A minimum of technical language makes this a very readable guide; includes the Indian and wildlife uses of the various species; key and informative introduction.

Petrides, George A. *A Field Guide to Trees and Shrubs*. (Boston: Houghton Mifflin, 1973). 646 species are presented, many with leaf and twig drawings which facilitate identification; key.

Steele, Frederic L. *Trees and Shrubs of Northern New England*. (Concord, N.H.: Society for the Protection of New Hampshire Forests, 1975). Concise descriptions of the major species of this area; illustrations.

## Chapter 8

### Katahdin from the East via Hunt's Farm

Avery, Myron H. "The Keep Path and Its Successors: The History of Katahdin from the West and North." *Appalachia*, December 1928, 132–147; June 1929, 224–237. Includes a detailed description of the Keep Path, which would have been Thoreau's route to the mountain in 1857 had he gone. A map shows the other routes from the east.

Avery, Myron H. "The Monument Line Surveyors on Katahdin." *Appalachia*, June 1928, 33–43. The fifth recorded ascent of Katahdin was made by surveyors, Joseph C. Norris and his son, in November 1825. They crossed the East Branch four miles above Hunt's, proceeding along what is now the Monument Line into the Northwest Basin, and from there turned south to reach the summit. Their descent, which approximated that of Thoreau, was to the east of Abol Slide to Abol Stream.

Avery, Myron H. "The Story of the Wassataquoik, A Maine Epic." *The Maine Naturalist*. September 1929, 83–96. An account of the lumbering operations on this river and its branches, and of the major forest fires of 1884 and 1903.

Blake, Joseph. "A Second Excursion to Mount Katahdin." *The Maine Naturalist*, June 1926, 74–83. Guided by the Rev. Keep, Blake ascended to Baxter Peak on July 4, 1856. His earlier trip, made in late July and early August of 1836, was from the south—up to West Branch and Abol Slide (see this issue, 71–73).

Hale, Edward Everett. "An Early Ascent of Katahdin." *Appalachia*, April 1901, 277–289. The 1845 Hale–Channing trip to Katahdin from the East Branch. An introduction is added to the original narrative, which appeared in the Boston *Daily Advertiser* of August 15, 1845.

Hamlin, Charles E. "Routes to Ktaadn." *Appalachia*, December 1881, 306–331. A description of the major approaches to the mountain, including that of Hunt's and Wassataquoik Stream. Hamlin (1825–1886) was Professor of Chemistry and Natural History at Colby College for twenty years until 1873, when he went to Harvard University as an assistant in the Museum of Comparative Zoology, a post which he held until his death; he also taught geography and geology at Harvard.

Henderson, Kenneth A., ed. "Penobscot East Branch in 1861 from the Diary and Letters of Alpheus Spring Packard." *Appalachia*, June 1951, 414–426. A. S. Packard Jr.

(1839–1905) was the entomologist on the 1861 Maine State Scientific Survey, which went up the East Branch to Matagamon and beyond to the Allagash and St. John rivers. Katahdin and the Traveler were climbed. The latter Avery believes was really Bald Mountain; see his "The Dead-Water Mountains," *The Maine Naturalist*, April 1930, 10–11.

Higginson, Thomas Wentworth. "Going to Mount Katahdin." *Putnam's Monthly Magazine*, September 1856, 242–255. Reprinted in *Appalachia*, June 1925, 101–129. A jocular rendition of Higginson's escorting five women to the mountain in 1855, discussed in the Afterword.

Hitchcock, Charles H., and Ezekiel Holmes, et al. "Preliminary Report upon the Natural History and Geology of the State of Maine. 1861." In the *Sixth Annual Report of the Secretary of the Maine Board of Agriculture. 1861.* (Augusta: Stevens & Sayward, Printers to the State, 1861). Report of the Maine Scientific Survey, which depicts the East Branch and other parts of Maine at the time of Thoreau.

Keep, Marcus R. "Mount Katahdin." *The Democrat*. Bangor, Maine. December 7, 1847. Keep (1816–1894) communicated this record of his ascent of the mountain to the newspaper on November 20, 1847. They reached the top on September 18, 1847, with snow on the ground and the noon temperature at 84° F. An altered version by one of the party, probably Rev. J. R. Munsell, appeared in John Springer's *Forest Life*, 193–205 (see Further Reading, Chapter 9).

Keep, Marcus R. "Mount Katahdin—Again." *The Democrat*. Bangor, Maine. October 9, 16, 23, 1849. The record of the first female expedition to the summit, which was led by Keep. The first woman to reach Baxter Peak was none other than Keep's wife, Hannah Taylor of Lincoln, whom he had married on July 29, 1849; the newlyweds stood on top August 20, 1849.

Laski, J. K. "Dr. Young's Botanical Expedition to Mount Katahdin." *The Maine Naturalist*, June 1927, 38–62. Reprinted from *Bangor Courier*, September 1847. An entertaining account of Dr. Young's ascent of Katahdin in August 1847, which was via Hunt's Farm where he stayed three nights. For more on Young, see Further Reading, Chapter 10.

Thurber, George. "Notes of an Excursion to Mount Katahdin." *The Maine Naturalist*, December 1926, 134–151. Reprinted from *Providence* (R.I.) *Journal*, September 26, 1847. Another account of Young's 1847 expedition by another of its members. Some biographical notes on Dr. Thurber are included in this issue as well, 171–174.

# About the Appalachian Mountain Club's Maine Woods Initiative

The Appalachian Mountain Club has launched the most ambitious conservation effort in its 132-year history—the Maine Woods Initiative. The Initiative is AMC's strategy for land conservation in the 100-Mile Wilderness region, combining outdoor recreation, resource protection, sustainable forestry, and community partnerships. It seeks to address the ecological and economic needs of the Maine Woods region by supporting local forest products jobs and traditional recreation, creating new multi-day recreational experiences for visitors, and attracting new nature-based tourism to the region.

A major component of the initiative is the AMC's purchase and management of 37,000 acres of forestland known as the Katahdin Iron Works (KIW) tract. The AMC also owns and operates Little Lyford Pond Camps and Medawisla Wilderness Camps, traditional Maine sporting camps with lodges and private cabins, that serve as a base for outdoor enthusiasts interested in hiking, paddling, fly-fishing, wildlife watching, and winter exploration by ski, snowshoe, or dogsled. AMC's property and sporting camps are open to the public. A third sporting camp, Gorman Chairback Camps, will open in the future. A trail network is being built to connect these camps for cross-country skiing, hiking, and mountain biking.

AMC's ultimate goal is linking together a 750,000-acre corridor of conserved land running from Greenville to Baxter State Park, creating a legacy comparable in size to the White Mountain National Forest.

For more information on the Maine Woods Initiative, visiting our sporting camps, and ways to support this project, see www.outdoors.org/mwi.

## About the Thoreau-Wabanaki Trail

The Thoreau-Wabanaki Trail is a project of Maine Woods Forever, which is dedicated to protecting the legacy of Maine's North Woods. The Trail is an initiative involving many people and groups interested in the historic, cultural, and spiritual aspects of Henry David Thoreau's Maine journeys, guided and influenced by the Penobscot Indians. For more information on the Trail, see: www.thoreauwabanakitrail.org. Maine Woods Forever can be reached at P.O. Box 692, Dover-Foxcroft, ME, or mainewoodsforever@yahoo.com.